NO-How Coaching

$

Also by Jim Collison

The Complete Suggestion Program Made Easy
The Complete Employee Handbook Made Easy
How to Protect Yourself and Your Business from Unemployment Rip-off
Cut and Control Employee-Related Costs: How to SLASH Payroll Costs
Skill-Building in Advanced Reading
Mental Power in Reading

NO-How Coaching

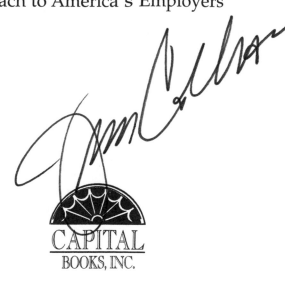

Strategies for Winning
in Sports and Business
from the Coach Who Says "No!"

Jim Collison
Coach to America's Employers

CAPITAL
BOOKS, INC.

Capital Books, Inc.
P.O. Box 605
Herndon, VA 20172-0605

ISBN 1-892123-72-X   (alk. paper)

Library of Congress Cataloging-in-Publication Data

Collison, Jim
    NO-how coaching: strategies for winning in sports and business from the coach who says "No!" / Jim Collison.
        p. cm.
    ISBN 1-892123-72-X
    1. Coaching (Athletics) 2. Mentoring I. Title.

GV711.C66 2001
796.07'7—dc21   2001037369

Printed in the United States of America on acid-free paper that meets the American National Standards Institute Z39-48 Standard.

First Edition

10 9 8 7 6 5 4 3 2 1

To John Gagliardi.
More than a great coach.
A good man.

ACKNOWLEDGMENTS

$\boxed{\$}$

To **John Gagliardi** for his generous and delightful sharing of time and memories.

To **Don Riley,** award-winning sports columnist for the *St. Paul Pioneer Press,* for his insights into John's NOs system and John's character. Don is co-author of *Gagliardi of St. John's* (out of print). Two of the quotes in this book are from Don's book.

To **Joe Engesser** for his NOODLES™ cartoons. As John Gagliardi says, "No surviving without plenty of humor."

To **Saint John's University,** for the use of the cover action photo and the photo of John Gagliardi. Saint John's was my home for four years and has been John's home for nearly 50 years. Long may its academic and athletic beacons shine.

FOREWORD

John Gagliardi, football coach of Saint John's University,
Collegeville, Minnesota

When coaches ask me about my NOs way of coaching, I'm inclined to tell them there's no secret to winning. Just DO it!

And when businesspeople ask me to speak to them about how we win and keep right on winning at Saint John's, I'm inclined to think, why me? Why ask me to give them any secrets on how to succeed in business? What we're doing with football is playing a game; we're having fun.

Then along comes Jim Collison. He's some kind of guru to employers. (He's a good friend and a Johnnie, too.)

First he tells me my NOs way of coaching has value for employers. And then he tells me he's going to write a book about them. He's lost it, I'm thinking.

> **[$/T]** John has always been up-to-date with the trends in college football. He's always playing the style of football good athletes want to play, no matter what that style happens to be at the time.
>
> —Dick Tressel, former football coach,
> Hamline University, St. Paul, Minn.

Before he and I are done talking and exploring this idea, though, I've added another 20 or so NOs to my list . . . and Jim has his book underway.

One of my 108 NOs is "No traditional drills" (#63)—pretty simple—only a few nontraditional drills and each has a purpose, like our Walk Away Drill.

Sometimes players get taunted and pushed, even slugged out there. The normal reaction is to strike back. And it's always the second guy, the one who strikes back, who gets the penalty. We say, "Do the smart thing, and just walk away. We want you in the game. Don't you want to stay in the game? Well, you're going to have to learn to walk away. Be a man; walk away from there. It's not a fight out there; it's a football game."

So in our Walk Away Drill we pair off. One player will hit the other across the helmet. The other . . . he walks away! It's simple.

Now, for all you coaches who want to know our *secrets* at Saint John's, read on.

And for all you employer-types who are curious about how anything we might do here can help your teams win, you read on, too.

John Gagliardi

> **[$/T]** At the end of the day, every great coach knows this: Players win games. Coaches don't win games.
>
> —Rick Majerus, University of Utah basketball coach

CONTENTS

$

Part III. NO-How Coaching and You

INTRODUCTION

How to Enjoy and Use This Book

$

$ Coaches help players develop into better players . . . Is it really so different with your team?

—Dave Worman, author, *Motivating Without Money*

About three years after John Gagliardi lost his cool following a game and blew up at an official, I asked him to comment on the incident. He'd made critical remarks about certain football officials after a game with the University of Saint Thomas, and John's boss, the Saint John's University president, insisted that John publicly apologize.

When I made a reference to the incident, John drew a blank. For seconds he did not recall it. When he did, he said, "You can criticize anybody. You can criticize the president, but not an official, not a collegiate official."

So I asked him, "What NO did you learn from the experience?"

"No remembering anything that was bad," he laughed.

And there it is on his NOs list—#91: "No dwelling on bad things."

> **[$]** Winning is not everything—but making the effort to
> win is.
>
> —Vince Lombardi, former Green Bay Packers coach

A list of NOs, in an age when YES is the socially acceptable word in our prosperous, permissive, and indulgent
culture? What's going on here? What's going on has been
going on with John Gagliardi's football teams for more than
50 years. And he's used his *anti-coaching* coaching strategies
to become the winningest active college football coach.

John Gagliardi, football coach at Saint John's University
in Collegeville, Minnesota, is just 31 wins away from
exceeding the 408-wins record of Eddie Robinson, former
football coach at Grambling State University.

NO-How Coaching is about how you can use John's NOs
in your own life and career . . . to win in coaching . . .
whether you are coaching in sports, coaching in the workplace, or both. Open this book at any page you choose. Skip
here and there in it. Or read it through from beginning to
end. Just as there is *NO single way to coach football* and *NO
being inflexible,* there's no single way to use this book.

Use these NOs to prompt your own creative juices. Be
unconventional. Ask yourself and your players or workplace associates: What can we do to break the mold? How
can we keep our competition off balance?

Jim Collison

$\$$ Part I $\$$

No End to the Winning

⊔$⊔ Chapter 1 ⊔$⊔

No Mission. Just Win.

⊔$⊔ It's just fun to play. That's why I keep coaching and it's why John keeps coaching.

—Frosty Westering, football coach, Pacific Lutheran College, after his team defeated Gagliardi's Saint John's team in a Division III quarterfinals playoff game (1999)

John Gagliardi's teams at Saint John's University in Collegeville, Minnesota, play football the way God means it to be played. With precision. With no wasted motion. With confidence. With elements of surprise. Even with, and maybe especially with, fun.

John once told Don Riley, sports writer for the *St. Paul Pioneer Press,* "the element of surprise is worth a twelfth player on the field."

John, now the winningest active college football coach, began surprising folks when he was 16—coaching his Trinidad, Colorado, Catholic High School football team in 1943. That's right, he started his coaching career at age 16 when the team's coach went off to war. With no adult male available to coach, the team and school scrambled for a solution. John was captain of the team and took on the role of coach.

$\lfloor\$\rfloor$ . . . The word *No!* itself is a very powerful release.
—Mary-Alice and Richard Jafolla in *The Simple Truth*

In the nearly 60 years since, John has kept right on surprising folks.

Through these years he's amassed a staggering list of 108 winning NOs that help explain how the coach of a small college in Minnesota can so consistently win against the odds. Not a list of goals and objectives. (John doesn't believe in them. It's a NO on his list, #18—"No goals needed. We just expect great things to happen.") Not even a playbook. (That's one of his NOs: #35.) His NOs help keep the minds of his players clear, uncluttered by pride and nonsense, and focused on their only mission: to win! (John doesn't even like the word *mission*. It's #20 on his list—"No `Mission Statement.' Just win.")

To win. Which his teams have done. Winning 377 games over 52 years, even scoring a one-season record in 1993 of an average of 61.5 points a game!

John Gagliardi's 58-year football coaching career is proof that nice guys can finish first. Proof that an ordinary guy can do extraordinary things. Proof that a contrarian can lead the way and win again and again. John's football coaching career places him near the pinnacle: just 31 wins away from the all-time winningest college football coaching title, currently held by Eddie Robinson of Grambling State University.

Some call him the anti-coach, because his approach to coaching over the years has defied the traditional, honored, almost sacred rules. For John's teams, it's no precision warm-up drills. No tackling in practices. No traditional calisthenics. No cheerleaders, God forbid!

> $ A coach in athletics parallels a boss in the working world. I've learned to accept the coach's advice, instruction and constructive criticism. Listening has made me a better athlete, and will probably make me a better employee.
>
> —Ann Knudtson, Evansville, Wisconsin, high school runner

At Saint John's University, John's football teams over the years have amassed an amazing record of NOs, adding to his list such NOs as: #99—"No discipline problems." #103—"No wider point margin in national playoff history." #104—"No team has fewer injuries." #106—"No small college team has had more national media coverage."

These NOs make up just some of his total list of 108 NOs that describe his guidelines (not rules, he'll tell you) and the results of his approach to winning football.

This book explains John's WINNING NOs, and explains their importance for winning in sports . . . and for winning in the work world.

John finds it hard to believe that his simple, focused, gentleman's coaching style would have any value to workplace leaders.

But consider some examples.

Start with the Golden Rule. "Just treat everyone the way you'd like to be treated. I tell the players to do everything you can to help the new guys. You don't get anywhere by being a jerk."

John was empowering his players long before *empowerment* became a workplace buzzword. Mention the word and he laughs. "You say 'empower' them. Hell! That's what we've been doing from day one."

His seasoned players, the older men, do most of the day-to-day coaching. They're the team leaders. "From day one, the seniors, the older guys, take over," he says. "They're the greeters, they run the drills. They teach the younger guys. That's why we get by with so few coaches."

No treating players like kids at Saint John's. No freshman or junior varsity program. No players cut. (He has as many as 165 players on his team, in a college of nearly 2,000 students. Saint John's is an all-male college, near St. Cloud, Minnesota.) No training table. No slogans. No pre-practice drills. "We only practice what we do in games," he says.

Motivate by treating people the way you want to be treated. "We don't drive players into the ground," he explains. For example, "We're the only team in history that eliminates all-out tackle in practice. So we've eliminated almost all practice injury. We haven't made a tackle on the practice field since '64 or '65. We try to eliminate the unnecessary."

Find the right people. "Where coaching really comes in is identifying the right people, the guys who will produce and be effective." (John does it with NO #3—"No athletic scholarships." And NO #4—"No recruiting off campus.") "Find the right people, show them what to do, then get the hell out of the way," he says. "And if they're not getting the job done, then your job is to find people to get the job done."

Always be ready to change. "We're always adjusting a little," John says. "We're pretty fluid. We don't even have a playbook. You always have to be ready to change." No playbook? "Well, each player gets his own stuff, so he gets his job done."

A culture of confidence in your people. "We want players who don't need rules. Who instinctively do the right thing," he says. It's really why his unorthodox coaching works. "The reason . . . confidence in what we're doing."

No focus on winning everything. John explains: "I know everyone prefers to be successful, to win. But we don't win every game. We're winning three out of four, but we're losing one out of four. And look at the plays. You lose most of your plays. Most great successes come after disaster. Good athletes don't give up. They bounce back."

Let the people doing the job make the decisions. "We let our quarterbacks call their own plays," John says. "They call 80, 90 percent of their own plays. Sure, I send in some plays. But if they don't like the play I send in, they don't have to use it. It's just a suggestion. And we led the nation in scoring with this system."

One of his quarterbacks said of John, "A coach that yells wouldn't get anything extra done. John treats us like men." Winning at coaching, in sports, or in work is like that. Treating people like adults.

$ Chapter 2 $

John Gagliardi's Coaching Records

$ **Good, Better, Best, Never let it rest.** Don't get
complacent. Push yourself out of your comfort zone
and set higher standards of achievement for yourself.
Once you've achieved a standard of excellence, never
let it rest—push yourself even higher.

—From *Famous Dave's*® "Lessons on Life from Famous Dave"

John Gagliardi is the winningest active coach in college
football. These are the highlights of his career as the 2001
football season opens.

- There have been more than 25,000 head coaches in the
  history of college football. At the start of the 2001 football season, the following seven coaches have won
  more than 300 games:

  Eddie Robinson   . . .408 games
  John Gagliardi   . . . .377 games
  Bear Bryant . . . . . . .323 games
  Joe Paterno . . . . . . .322 games
  Pop Warner . . . . . . .319 games
  Bobby Bowden . . . .315 games
  Alonzo Stagg   . . . . .314 games

- John is the second winningest coach of all time. He
  needs only 31 more wins to become the all-time win-

ningest college football coach. Among those still coaching, he ranks first. Only he, Paterno, and Bowden are still active.

- As the 2000 football season reached its national climax, Saint John's lost the national championship in the final second of the game, 10–7. John's teams have won three national championships and 24 conference titles and have ranked nationally 37 of the past 39 years. They were ranked second in 2000.
- Saint John's led the nation three times each in scoring and in defense.
- In 1993, the team scored an average of 61.5 points per game, setting a record that may never be broken—the only team ever to score more than 700 points in one season.

Here are more highlights of John's coaching career:

- He started coaching high school football (at Trinidad, Colorado, Catholic High School) at age 16.
- In his six years coaching high school, his teams won four conference titles.
- He coached at Carroll College in Helena, Montana, after graduating from Colorado College in 1949. In his first four seasons as a college coach, he led Carroll to three conference titles.
- At Saint John's University, Collegeville, Minnesota, in his early years he coached track and hockey in addition to football.
- His hockey teams, in five seasons, compiled a 42–25–1 record, even though John never played hockey a day in his life. His hockey teams' record is still the best career winning percentage of any hockey coach in the school's history.

| $ | John's mother lived until she was 98. Now John says, "If I can hang in there another 16 years all I have to win is about 2 games a year" for the all-time winningest coach title.

- John's college football coaching career record: 377–109–11 (1949–2000)
- Most points scored in season: 702 (1993)
- Longest winning streak: 20 games (1962–1964)
- Biggest margin of victory: 75–2 vs. Coe College (1991)
- Minnesota Intercollegiate Athletic Conference (MIAC) championships: 20
- National championships: 3 (1963, 1965, 1976)
- Years without a losing season: 33 (1968 to present)
- Least points allowed in a season: 27 (1965)
- Ranked #18 in *Sports Illustrated*'s 50 Greatest Sports Figures from Minnesota: 1900–2000

⟂$⟂ **Chapter 3** ⟂$⟂

Winning with NOs

The List in John's Order

$ The great ones, in every area, in anything, football, employees, anybody, are guys who were able to accept and bounce back from bad breaks, bad news.

—John Gagliardi

Year-by-year John Gagliardi has added to his list of NOs. Now his list is up to 108! Following is John's list, in the order he's prepared it.

THE PREFACE

1. *No single way to coach football.*
2. *No worrying about being different or unique.*

THE OVERALL PROGRAM

3. *No athletic scholarships.*
4. *No recruiting off campus.*
5. *No big staff . . . four assistant coaches.*
6. *No freshman or junior varsity program.*
7. *No insisting on being called "Coach."*
8. *No players cut.*
9. *No pampering athletes.*

$ But couple "Don't Quit," and "Just Do It," and you got
  the complete success formula in five economical words. It
  has been said that the only real failure comes from
  quitting before the job is done. If that is true, you can
  guarantee a successful outcome by vowing never to quit.

  —Paul Lemberg in *Faster Than the Speed of Change*

---

10. *No one persuaded to come out or stay out.*
11. *No Hall of Fame.*
12. *No outlawing of high school letter jackets or T-shirts.*
13. *No hazing tolerated.*
14. *No creating busy work. Eliminate the unnecessary.*
15. *No changing our belief we must eliminate the unnecessary.*
16. *No faltering in preparing to being brilliant in the basics.*
17. *No lack of attention to fundamentals and the little things.*
18. *No goals needed. We just expect great things to happen.*
19. *No depending on good luck. Only bad luck can hinder us.*
20. *No "Mission Statement." Just win.*
21. *No problems or obstacles can stop us.*
22. *No being inflexible.*
23. *No surviving without plenty of humor.*

THE SEASON

24. *No traditional captains. All seniors rotate this honor.*
25. *No rules except the Golden Rule.*

> |$| Whenever you are asked if you can do a job, tell 'em, "Certainly, I can!" Then get busy and find out how to do it.
>
> —Theodore Roosevelt

26. *No one wanted except those who don't need rules. Those who need rules won't keep them.*
27. *No one wanted except those who do the right thing. We will surround them with others just like them.*
28. *No staff meetings.*
29. *No player meetings.*
30. *No special dormitory.*
31. *No training table. Team eats with other students.*
32. *No dress code.*
33. *No nicknames unless complimentary.*
34. *No superstitions.*
35. *No playbooks.*
36. *No statistics posted.*
37. *No newspaper clippings posted, ours or theirs.*
38. *No excuses.*
39. *No denying responsibility for own actions.*
40. *No blaming anyone else for your or their mistakes.*
41. *No tolerating loud-mouths, braggarts, or show-offs.*

THE PRACTICES

42. *No resemblance to a BOOT CAMP.*
43. *No compulsory film sessions except Monday (only day team looks at films).*
44. *No practice on Sunday or Monday.*

> **$** I've been fighting since I was eight years old and I've
> made mistakes all my life. The most important thing is
> to correct the mistakes.
>
> —Evander Holyfield, WBA-IBF heavyweight
> boxing champion (1999)

45. *No long practices: 90 minutes Tuesday,
    Wednesday, Thursday; 30–45 minutes on Friday.*
46. *No practice schedule posted.*
47. *No posting anything on bulletin board except
    travel information and kicking teams.*
48. *No practice pants issued. Shorts or sweats worn
    at all practices.*
49. *No agility drills.*
50. *No lengthy calisthenics (about four minutes of
    stretching).*
51. *No calisthenics when Daylight Savings time
    ends. Darkness limits practice to 30 minutes.*
52. *No pre-practice drills. Players are on their own.*
53. *No practice apparatus or gadgets.*
54. *No blocking sleds.*
55. *No blocking or tackling dummies.*
56. *No tackling.*
57. *No whistles.*
58. *No laps.*
59. *No wind sprints.*
60. *No yelling or screaming at players.*
61. *No getting in player's face.*
62. *No water or rest denied when players want it.*
63. *No traditional drills.*
64. *No practice modules.*
65. *No underclassmen carry equipment other than
    their own.*

> $ Failure is good. It's fertilizer. Everything I've learned,
> I've learned from making mistakes.
>
> —Rick Pitino, former head basketball coach, University of
> Kentucky, president and head coach, Boston Celtics

66. *No spring practice.*
67. *No practice outside in rain, excessive heat, cold, or threat of lightning.*
68. *No practice outside if mosquitoes or gnats are bad.*
69. *No practice under lights to get ready for an away night game.*

THE GAMES

70. *No "Big" game we point to.*
71. *No grading films.*
72. *No special pre-game meals.*
73. *No scripted plays.*
74. *No print handouts given to players.*
75. *No big deal when we score. We expect to score.*
76. *No Gatorade® celebrations.*
77. *No trying to "kill" opponent.*
78. *No trash talk tolerated.*
79. *No tendency charts.*
80. *No computer analysis.*
81. *No coaches on phones in press box.*
82. *No player unsuited at home.*
83. *No player NOT played in routs. (Over 150 have played many times.)*
84. *No cheap shots tolerated.*
85. *No belief that aggressive teams get penalties.*
86. *No counting tackles. We play a team defense.*

> $ Good shooting [in basketball] is unforced, effortless technical virtuosity.
>
> —John Fitzsimmons Mahoney in *The Tao of the Jump Shot: An Eastern Approach to Life and Basketball*

87. *No precision pre-game drills.*
88. *No precision huddles.*
89. *No cheerleaders.*
90. *No special post-game meals.*

THE OFF-SEASON

91. *No dwelling on bad things.*
92. *No meetings.*
93. *No captains' practice.*
94. *No guest speaker for football banquet. Seniors do the honor.*
95. *No study or tutoring necessary.*
96. *No compulsory weight program.*

THE RESULTS

97. *No player has NOT graduated. (Almost all in four years.)*
98. *No player lost through ineligibility.*
99. *No discipline problems.*
100. *No senior class has NOT had a prospective pro football player.*

> $ Nothing is particularly hard if you divide it into small jobs.
>
> —Henry Ford

⌊$⌋ Keep your mental muscle loose. You have to keep
 ⊤ stretching.

> —Leslie Wexner, founder, chairman,
> president, and CEO of The Limited, Inc.

101. *No senior class has NOT had players accepted*
     to medical, law, or other graduate schools.
102. *No other college team in history averaged*
     61.5 points a game—the NCAA record.
103. *No wider point margin in national playoff*
     history.
104. *No team has fewer injuries.*
105. *No small college coach has won more games*
     (second most in history).
106. *No small college team has had more national*
     media coverage.
107. *No promises. Just results.*
108. *No end to the possibilities of more NOs.*

⌊$⌋ When I play, I'm singing words inside me. I put all of
 ⊤ myself into it. I play from the heart. If you don't,
   where's the joy?

> —Debra Saylor, pianist, finalist in the Van Cliburn
> International Piano Competition for amateurs (2000)

⌊$⌋ Part II ⌊$⌋

Winning NOs in Sports and in the Workplace

John Gagliardi's NOs Grouped by Topic

$\lfloor$\$$\rfloor$ Chapter 4 $\lfloor$\$$\rfloor$

No Single Best Way

$\lfloor$\$$\rfloor$ If we worried about being unique we'd be in trouble.
We're different. We know it. We're not looking for
converts. We're just comfortable doing what we're
doing.

—John Gagliardi

---

1. *No single way to coach football.*
22. *No being inflexible.*

In Sports

John Gagliardi learned a valuable lesson from his mother.
"An Italian mother, maker of great spaghetti," he says.
John's wife, Peggy, tried to learn how to make spaghetti by
watching his mother. But every time his mother made it,
she made it differently. After a while, Peggy asked her
mother-in-law why she made it differently each time.
Peggy told her mother-in-law, "Last time you used this.
This time you used that. Why?" John's mother replied,
"Well, that's what I had in the house."

"That's the way you've got to coach," John says. "It
depends on what you have." You can't be rigid if you don't
have certain talent. "If you've got good passers, you throw

the ball. If you don't have good passers, you don't throw the ball."

Always be ready to change. "We're always adjusting a little. We're pretty fluid. We don't ever have a playbook. You always have to be ready to change."

In the Workplace

The pool of talent in the workplace, especially for exceptional talent, is tight and will get even tighter in the future. So we workplace leaders have to adapt our own talents, and the talents of our people, to the challenges we have.

There is no single best way to lead people.

Forget trying to stay with and get ahead of the latest paradigm shift (whatever that is). Forget trying to mimic the newest, cutting-edge psycho-babble workplace cultural change. Don't waste too much time trying to copy the success methods of your competitors.

The world is moving at fiber-optic speed. I tell employers who voice workplace and business challenges, who are looking for magic solutions from high-priced experts: "Look to the brains of your own people. Within your workforce are all of, or certainly most of, the answers you need."

The strategies you develop to win won't be cookie cutter strategies. You and your people will experience the pride of succeeding with your own creative talents and skills.

$\lfloor\$\rfloor$ Chapter 5 $\lfloor\$\rfloor$

No Fear of Being Different

$\lfloor\$\rfloor$ All great managers seem to have one thing in common: They don't hesitate to break virtually every rule held sacred by conventional wisdom.

—Workforce magazine, June 1999

---

2. No worrying about being different or unique.

In Sports

"Anti-coaching": That's what one journalist wrote about Saint John's football and John Gagliardi's system. Other journalists and sports analysts have called his approach to coaching *contrarian.*

John's coaching system—his NOs list—is unique. As he says, "We don't follow the herd." Asked if he thinks he's a contrarian, he laughs and says, "I just figure if we're unique, that's good. We just do what we think is right." And he never worries about it.

In the Workplace

Be unique. Have no fear of breaking the rules.

Harley-Davidson is prospering by breaking rules. At Harley's newest plant outside Kansas City, Missouri,

425 hourly and salaried employees assemble all the Sport-ster motorcycles and about 25% of all the motorcycles made by Harley, using a radical plant-leadership democracy model. Every Harley employee is on a team (at Harley the teams are called groups). Every team helps run the plant. The plant manager, Karl Eberle, shares his cubicle with two union presidents. When Eberle leaves town, the union presidents share in the leadership of the plant.

Don't pay too much heed to those who tell you, "You can't do it that way. We tried that three years ago and it didn't work. Our competitor tried that five years ago and nearly went broke."

Be creative. Look for the unique way for yourself and for your business or organization.

⌊$⌋ **Chapter 6** ⌊$⌋

No Throwing Away Money

⌊$⌋ The illiterate of the 21st century will not be those who cannot read and write, but those who cannot learn, unlearn, and relearn.

—Alvin Toffler, author, *Future Shock* and *The Third Wave*

---

3. No athletic scholarships.

In Sports

True, when John started coaching at Saint John's in 1953 the football program had scholarships. The Benedictine monks of the university, interviewing him for the coaching position, asked him, "Do you need scholarships to win?" The monks wanted a winning team, but they were reluctant to part unnecessarily with dollars. John remembers telling the monks he didn't think he needed scholarships to win. "Oh, God, I could see I had the job right there."

The NCAA Division III today doesn't allow scholarships. But for many years John coached his team to winning seasons and championships against teams using scholarships.

$| Studies prove that when people are thinking about
how much they're going to get for what they're doing,
they tend to choose the easiest possible task. When you
remove rewards, when you get rid of extrinsic
motivators, people are more likely to want to challenge
themselves.

—Alfie Kohn, author of *Punished by Rewards: The Trouble
with Gold Stars, Incentive Plans, A's, Praise and Other Bribes*

About athletic scholarships, John says, "Athletic welfare is what I call it. I've always liked that we turn out good,
good students who're also good athletes."

In the Workplace

The ideal is no bribing employees and no overpaying
employees to work for you. The ideal is to create a workplace where challenges and opportunities attract—and
keep—the best people. Simply paying out more money in
wages, salaries, and bonuses is your least effective way to
build and retain a high-quality workforce.

Recently I analyzed six surveys and studies that in a
variety of ways sought to learn what employees want most.
Compensation didn't rank first in any of them. Earnings
potential ranked second in one, third in one, and fourth in
one. Look at what employees valued most (ranked first) in
the six surveys and studies: respect from the manager, full
appreciation, positive work environment, outside training,
and opportunity for advancement, training, and mentoring.

I recently had a salesperson who consistently underper-
formed. Each time I talked with her about what she
believed she needed to perform at the level we both knew
she could, she would say she needed more money, higher

bonuses, so I switched her to a straight commission plan. She could easily earn more simply by selling more. What happened? She continued producing at the same level but concentrated her selling in three or four days a week and took off one or two days a week. What really motivated her was not more money. What motivated her was flex time and more time off.

Study after study shows that money isn't all that employees want and that money isn't a good motivator for most employees.

In three studies in 1987–1988, asking employees and managers to rank rewards and motivators in order of importance, money never ranked first. It was fifth in a George Mason University study, fourth in an American Productivity and Quality Center study, and third in a Gannett News Service poll.

Fast forward to 2000 and a global study of what it takes to retain talented employees. Accenture, formerly Andersen Consulting, interviewed nearly 500 senior executives from firms in eight countries on three continents and spanning 10 major industry groups. One finding: Most employers continue to struggle with retention because they are relying on salary increases and bonuses to prevent turnover. A second finding: Leading employers provide employees with a comprehensive range of career and skills-development opportunities.

Also in 2000, Development Dimensions International (DDI)—a Bridgeville, Pennsylvania, firm—queried employees of major corporations chosen as "benchmark" organizations about their level of job satisfaction. When employees ranked what was most important, money was only the fifth most important value. The most important values were, in order: the ability to balance work and outside life, the meaningfulness of work, trust among employees, and the employees' relationship with their supervisor or manager.

Obviously, more money isn't everything for most employees.

$\lfloor$\$$\rfloor$ Chapter 7 $\lfloor$\$$\rfloor$

No Putting Outside Recruiting First

$\lfloor$\$$\rfloor$ I look for a guy who has a passion to excel and it's not motivated by his contract. It's something in his background, his mom or his dad, that helped him develop.

—Dick Vermeil, head coach, St. Louis Rams

---

4. No recruiting off campus.

In Sports

While other coaches and their staffs are investing time, money, and energy chasing after stars, John is giving prospective freshmen the welcome on campus. How does he recruit winning athletes without scouring his Minnesota–Northern Iowa–Dakota territory for the best and actively courting them? With his winning program!

John doesn't especially seek out the most outstanding high school athletes. Instead, he's looking for students with scholastic ability, willingness to learn. "Give me a mediocre athlete with responsibility and desire to learn and the willingness to improve in the classroom, and I'll show you a man who can become a valuable asset to any team."

John makes use of the talent that shows up. Any Saint John's student can join the team. Says John: "We get young men who want to think, who want to improve and who want to test their ingenuity and intelligence and judgment in tough situations."

In the Workplace

Sure, in today's extremely tight labor market, we have to recruit aggressively for good talent. We have to be imaginative and recruit in as many ways as we can. If we can afford it, it means spending time and money going "off campus" to job fairs and to colleges and universities.

But if we have a winning, attractive workplace and work culture, the good applicants will seek us out. Saving us time and money. And assuring us that we're hiring people who *want* to be with us.

Want to improve your recruiting? Ask your best, most recent new hires what they like best about working for you. Then include these features and benefits in your recruiting ads. At Employers of America, we discovered that "a pleasant workplace" and "a fun place to work" are even more attractive than the pay scale. We can't beat the pay scales of our competitors in our area, so in our recruiting ads we play up the "soft," human benefits.

Before recruiting for the best people by offering the highest pay and the most costly benefits, ask yourself: What are some no-cost and low-cost benefits and perks we can offer that will attract the best people? Opportunity and a record of success will be at or near the top of your list.

⌐$⌐ **Chapter 8** ⌐$⌐

No Top-Heavy Staff

⌐$⌐ The ability to coach yourself is critical. Sixty percent of coaching others is the ability to coach yourself.

—Tom Gegax, CEO, Tires Plus, author
of *Winning in the Game of Life*

---

5. No big staff . . . four assistant coaches.

In Sports

For years, John was it. No assistants. As he talks about it, he again mentions the monks of Saint John's who hired him. "They didn't believe in a lot of spending." When he was on campus applying for the coaching position, he looked up John (Johnny Blood of Green Bay Packers fame) McNally, the coach he would be replacing. McNally cited the frugal monks and warned John Gagliardi that he couldn't win at Saint John's. "Nobody can win here consistently." But John and his teams did win. And win consistently.

In the early years, coaching without assistants, John had to learn all facets of the game. He learned to depend on players to use their own instincts. He delegated to players. He learned to use his experienced players as his assistants.

He lets players teach players. He polishes 18 or 20 veteran men, who pass on the techniques to another 18 or 20 less experienced men, and in a week the whole team of 160–plus men are trained. John needs no big staff of assistants because he lets his veterans pass on the lessons they've learned.

In the Workplace

John may have been the first "boss" in America to empower his "employees." Maybe the first in the world. I'm exaggerating, but not by much. (Jesus Christ empowered his team. He even put his team in charge!) But John certainly was one of the pioneers of empowerment, long before the word was popularized.

Employees actually run some businesses and organizations. One example: the Foldcraft Company in Kenyon, Minnesota. Steve Sheppard is the CEO. But the 225 employees own 100% of the firm, which manufactures restaurant furniture. Sheppard doesn't run the company, and he can't hide. Sheppard says that he's running *with* the workforce and not hiding a thing.

For the first few years, the employees met together monthly (in the local Catholic Church) to review the firm's financial, production, and profit numbers. In 1998, the meetings of all employees together went from monthly to quarterly. Between the quarterly meetings, the managers meet weekly "to project where we think we will be in the next two or three months, where we are today, and where we'll be in the next month," Sheppard explains. Then the managers meet weekly with their employees to share information and discuss what has to be done to meet the goals.

Says Sheppard of the Foldcraft team and culture: ". . . We're trying to help people to understand, person-by-person, how they contribute to the welfare of the company, hour-by-hour. One focus now is to help people understand the cause and effect of this effort on the company's bottom line. If the game is helping the company make money, to be healthy, to raise the stock value . . . it's important to me to know what my contribution to the game is, hour-by-hour."

An example of the payoff at Foldcraft: In 1993, the firm's workers' comp was costing $400,000 annually. The workforce made that a focus of their efforts. In 1998, the annual workers' comp premium was running less than $80,000, a savings of over $300,000 a year!

NOODLES™

⌊$⌋ **Chapter 9** ⌊$⌋

No Artificial Limits on Talent

⌊$⌋ God gives everybody talents, and you should try at a young age to figure out your talent. Not everybody has the same one. Then you should use your talent or talents to the very greatest extent you can in the few years God gives you on this little planet.

—Sir John Templeton

---

6. *No freshman or junior varsity program.*

In Sports

When a young man about to select a college asks John, "Do you have a freshman (JV football) program?" John answers, "Would you rather be on a JV team or would you rather be on the varsity?" John wants all the men interested in playing to be part of the varsity squad. "We're all together, all one, big family. . . . We don't have separate families here, we're just one, big family."

Impressive? Believe it! "We all suit up for the home games. We don't play separately," John says. "We want guys who think they can play with the varsity."

In the Workplace

The key word in the previous sentence is *think*. "We want guys who *think* they can play with the varsity."

That's what you want on your workplace team. You want employees and associates who think—who *believe*—"they can play with the varsity."

When I'm hiring someone, I focus on the applicant's work behavior style, proven abilities, past achievements, and brain power. These four show me the applicant's *potential*. I don't pay too much attention to work experiences, unless these experiences demonstrate an applicant's work ethic and potentials. I want people with the potential and the desire—the brainpower and the will to use it—to play with the varsity, to play with the first team.

What about young people, fresh out of high school or college? Are they ready for the first team? Some are. Absolutely. And you will never know unless you give them the chance to prove it.

⌊$⌋ Chapter 10 ⌊$⌋

No Need to Discipline

⌊$⌋ With self-discipline most anything is possible.

—Theodore Roosevelt

---

99. *No discipline problems.*

In Sports

Reading the sports section in your daily paper is like reading a police report. The coach's job description in many schools and colleges, and with many professional teams, includes "chief disciplinarian." Not at Saint John's. John doesn't believe in job descriptions and he doesn't have discipline problems.

What's his secret? "We get good kids," he explains. "We want guys who don't need rules. People who need rules, they aren't going to keep 'em anyway. We want guys that don't need job descriptions."

> $ I tell my son sometimes: Grow up to be a man. It's a
> waste of time to grow up to be a boy.
>
> —Leonard Pitts, columnist, Knight Ridder/Tribune

This is interesting, John's tying his team's good conduct to the idea of no job descriptions. What's the connection? John remembers when he was athletic director, having to hire other staff. "I always found the same thing. The guy that says, 'Well, it's not in my job description,' he was worthless. Completely worthless."

So John always is looking for the young men who don't need rules.

In the Workplace

I don't think John really is talking about job descriptions and rules here. He's talking about *character*. Young people in sports and people in the workplace who have *character* don't turn into discipline problems.

At the time Atlanta Braves star pitcher John Rocker ran off from the mouth and insulted foreigners, homosexuals, and African Americans in New York, Cubs coach Billy Williams, noting Rocker's pitching skill and speculating on the possibility that Atlanta might jettison Rocker, told the press: "Yes, some team will pick him up. Winning baseball games has gone far beyond whether this guy is a good guy or not. As long as he can pitch . . . they are going to look beyond what he said and did. Winning has become so much more important today than looking at the character of the individual."

So what's the secret of no (or at least few) discipline problems in the workplace? Employ people with good character. And, like John Gagliardi, have high expectations. Hire people who don't need rules!

$ Chapter 11 $

No Reverence for Titles

> $ As we have transformed a family business into a modern one, we have tried to preserve the best of what my father and grandfather created. There is a family feeling in the company that's difficult to describe. We don't care much about [corporate] title and hierarchy. Family life and the company's business spill over into each other.
>
> —Victor Fung, of Hong Kong's Li & Fung Ltd., quoted in Ming-Jer Chen's book *Inside Chinese Business: A Guide for Managers Worldwide*

7. *No insisting on being called "Coach."*

In Sports

"I hate that," John says. "Other coaches just love to call each other coach, coach. Coach this, coach that. They can't call you by your first name. We're different here."

John's attitude probably began when, as a student in high school, he coached his high school football team. Little wonder he grew into his adulthood comfortable with "John" and uncomfortable with "Coach." "In a business organization," he notes, "I don't think everybody's calling themselves 'Foreman.' To me it's ridiculous."

> $ It is hard, if not impossible, to attach importance to
> another person or to someone else's task if we can't get
> the focus off of ourselves. . . . Know your place as a
> leader. If you humble yourself to your team, your sense
> of importance will be heightened and your team's will
> skyrocket.
>
> —Adele B. Lynn, in *In Search of Honor:
> Lessons from Workers on How to Build Trust*

John's attitude on this reflects his belief that he's far more than a football coach. More than that, he's a teacher and a molder of men. He encourages each player to introduce himself to all the other players and to learn the other players' names (that's on a team with 160 or more players). It's part of teaching them to gain confidence in themselves, in an adult world.

And speaking of players and not wanting to be called Coach, John says, "I don't call them 'player' do I?"

In the Workplace

I'm uncomfortable with titles. I've got plenty of them. I'm president of three corporations, chairman of another, and senior editor of a newsletter. Whew! But when someone asks me what my title is—or "What do you do there?"— more often than not I joke, "Chief cook and bottle washer."

I suppose my relaxed attitude toward titles and names began with my hearing my dad tell people, "I don't care what people call me, just as long as they call me for dinner." I had an educator friend (in fact, we co-authored an elementary textbook together) who went away for a time to get his doctorate. When he returned, I was a bit chagrined because he wanted everyone (including me) to call him "Doctor."

Titles are important motivators for some people. But workplace leaders—executives, managers, supervisors, team leaders—gain more with employees and team members in today's workplace by downplaying rank. Demanding respect from employees—rather than earning it—turns off employees, creating resentment and depressing performance.

Where should you put the emphasis? Consider the findings from Adele B. Lynn's interviews with 1,000 workers. She is founder of Lynn Learning Labs, Belle Vernon, Pennsylvania, and author of *In Search of Honor: Lessons from Workers on How to Build Trust.*

In her book, Lynn lists numerous "Spirit Killers and Soul Suckers" that are guaranteed to kill employees' spirit and get less from them. At the top of the list: "Display a Celebrity ego."

Here and there a few employers are even scrapping titles. Consider Johnsonville Foods, in Kohler, Wisconsin (maker of bratwurst and bologna). At Johnsonville titles are out. Have been for years. Employees are called members. Sales went from $15 million to $130 million in just nine years. Wal-Mart employs associates. Target employs team members. At Burley Design Cooperative in Eugene, Oregon, the workers own the business. No one in the place has a title.

The best title for a workplace coach? Coach is fine. Just don't insist on it.

$ Chapter 12 $

No Ignoring Anyone's Talent

$ We've tried to put everybody in the game a lot of
times. . . . That's their one moment in glory. . . . We
do it because we just think it's the human thing to do.
As long as they're on the team we're going to treat 'em
that way.

—John Gagliardi

---

8. *No players cut.*
10. *No one persuaded to come out or stay out.*
82. *No player unsuited at home.*
83. *No player NOT played in routs. (Over 150 have
played many times.)*

In Sports

What a sight! A Johnnies' home game on a bright, sunny
fall afternoon. A crisp breeze. Suddenly a huge wave of
young men in cardinal (red) and white uniforms and hel-
mets comes pouring onto the football field. Nowhere else in
sports will you see this. At least 150 young men—sometimes 160 or more—are suited and are taking over the field!

How is this possible? Simple. At Saint John's, any student can come out for football. And no players are cut.

"We're like a big family," John says.

John recruits hard, but without offering money (scholarships). And he doesn't leave campus to recruit. Mostly, he and his small staff let the team's winning history attract the students who have a burning desire to join the Saint John's family.

And in routs, every player plays. Imagine it. More than 150 men have played in the same game, many times!

How's that for rewarding every player who comes out?

In the Workplace

Obviously, in your workplace, sometimes you have to do some cutting. But the ideal is to do such a good job of recruiting and hiring people, and then such a good job of training and motivating these stars, that you won't have to terminate them. Make terminating an employee your last option, not your first. And, obviously, coaches can't tolerate underperformance.

Your challenge as a coach in the workplace is to create the conditions that bring out the best in people. It's not to set up people for failure. It's to set them up for winning. It's easy to do, but it takes time and patience. I once had a vice president who started work in an entry-level clerical position. She had no college degree. What she had was exceptional talent, attention to detail, and persistence. Whatever I asked her to do, she tried.

She is just one of the many employees I've had over the years who have proven me right—that when I've hired potential, brains, and desire, I've rarely had to cut.

|$| Chapter 13 |$|

No Spoiling Your Team with Unearned Favors

> |$| I'm not here as a social worker. I'm not a clergyman trying to save souls. I just want to have good people surrounded by other good people so we're all comfortable and don't alienate the hell out of each other.
>
> —John Gagliardi (quoted in the *Richmond Times-Dispatch* column by Paul Woody)

9. *No pampering athletes.*
30. *No special dormitory.*
31. *No training table. Team eats with other students.*
72. *No special pre-game meals.*
90. *No special post-game meals.*

In Sports

When John started as coach at Saint John's, he took over a traditional system that in several ways pampered the athletes and set them apart.

The team had its own dining room, separate from all the other students. "They even were served extra milk!" John remembers. "After a year I said, 'I don't want these guys to have that [special treatment] because what do the rest of

---

⌊$⌋ Sports do not build character. They reveal it.

—Heywood Hale Broun, American broadcast journalist
and sports correspondent with CNS news

---

the students think of these guys.' " The monks liked that and his players liked it. "I said I want them to be just like the rest of the students."

And nothing special to eat on the road. "We give 'em a couple of choices. We either have a ham sandwich or a chicken sandwich. Something like that. They don't like it, they don't have to eat it." He chuckles when he says that.

In the Workplace

You're a leader and a coach, not a circus ring master, bribing with candy, not a pampering parent.

A major challenge for workplace leaders today is retaining employees. In a tight labor market, many employers are engaged in contortionist-like efforts to attract and then keep employees, just to keep turnover below 50% to 100% a year.

A consultant who works with nursing homes called me, seeking help with his challenge. "They're all telling me that turnover among their employees is their biggest problem. What can I offer them that will help them cut their turnover?" As we talked, it was clear that he was looking for a quick fix, a magic pill. He was looking for a simple, one-day, three-step action plan for management . . . or for one or two cheap new employee benefits to offer.

But there isn't a quick and easy approach to attracting good employees and keeping them. Piling up more treats in your benefits package isn't the answer. Bribing applicants and pampering them after you hire them isn't the answer.

> [$] The best people understand that you can't be successful
>   without sacrifice. The best never complain about
>   sacrifices—they're proud of them.
>
>   —Lou Holtz, head football coach at the University of South
>   Carolina and former head football coach at Notre Dame

On the same day that the nursing home consultant called me, I was talking with Curt Coffman, who is global practice leader with The Gallup Organization's Workplace Management Practice and co-author of *First Break All the Rules*. Gallup recently had released results of a study showing that one of every five U.S. employees is *actively disengaged* from their work. They're physically present at work but emotionally and mentally retired.

As we talked about how actively disengaged employees get hired and develop in a workplace, Coffman made a telling observation. The fault for having so many actively disengaged employees in a workplace often lies squarely with the leader, with the supervisor who does the hiring and has day-to-day contact with the employees. The leader screws up in hiring. The leader abuses and turns off the employees.

Improving retention of good employees and improving performance of employees don't begin with and don't rely on pampering them with unearned or unwanted benefits. It begins with hiring the right people for the right jobs, and it continues with treating them fairly and coaching them, so that they perform as motivated, responsible adults.

And definitely, don't pamper your stars. Give everyone opportunities to win and challenge everyone to demonstrate that they can accept more responsibility.

Our activities and our lives are moving at fiber-optic speed. Bill Gates has a book out titled *Business @ the Speed of Thought*, focusing managers on succeeding in this fast-emerging digital, e-business economy. Frankly, to win in the workplace, no one can stagnate. No one can rest on his or her laurels. And no coach who wants to win can risk pampering employees.

Morris R. Shechtman, Los Angeles, an employee retention and development strategist and chairman of The Schechtman Group, even advises *against* hiring the perfect applicant. Say what? He notes "today's rapidly changing, information-intensive, global business environment" and says we "should be hiring employees who don't quite fit."

These employees don't even want to be pampered.

⊥$⊥ Chapter 14 ⊥$⊥

No Limiting Recognition to a Few

⊥$⊥ This new hall of fame might stand as a beacon to smart
kids who are good at sport, reminding them that
games are great fun, but they should not be
substituted for lasting achievement.

> —Donald Kaul, former *Des Moines Register* columnist,
> commenting on the International Scholar-Athlete Hall of
> Fame on the campus of the University of Rhode Island

---

11. *No Hall of Fame.*

In Sports

No special recognition for the stars. This is contrary to all
the ways of our ego-obsessed culture. Not shining the spot-
light on the stars certainly is contrary to the hero obsession
of big college sports and pro sports. For John, though, not
making heroes out of individuals makes sense. "There's so
many players who deserve it [the fame]. But with the Hall
of Fame mentality, it's limited. Here, we would never be
able to get all the guys who deserve it in there."

John continues: "I think it's very unfair. Football's very
much a team sport. Even when we're leading the nation,
statistically, we won't ever put it all on the board that this
quarterback, or runner, is leading the nation. Because it
takes a lot of people, like the linemen, to make it happen."

> [$] So when you're out there on the court, I want you to
> be asking each moment, "What's the best thing I can
> do right now to help the team?" . . . This game is
> about the guy who makes the good pass, the rebound,
> the defensive stop, just as much as it is about the guy
> who makes the basket.
>
> —Andrew Bard Schmookler, basketball
> coach to 10- and 11-year-old boys

In the Workplace

I heard on the radio a report that most people are suspicious of the wealthy. Something about a survey that showed 80%, or some such high percentage, of respondents believe that the wealthy are greedy and selfish. There's something perverse in human nature that causes people to resent the success of others.

In your workplace, when you focus attention on stars, you risk extinguishing the enthusiasm of all the nonstars and aspiring stars. Actually, if you are hiring good people and coaching them well, everyone in your workplace can star.

What to do? Spread recognition around. Give everyone opportunities to achieve, and acknowledge their success when they do succeed.

Instead of having *a* hall of fame *in* your workplace, make your *entire workplace* a hall of fame. Help everyone in your hall of fame know they are—or can be—a star.

NOODLES™

Copyright © 1994 Employers of America. NOODLES is a trademark of Employers of America.

$ Chapter 15 $

No Narrow-Minded Dress Rules

$ Those teams that have been most successful are the ones that have demonstrated the greatest commitment to their people. They are the ones that have created the greatest sense of belonging.

—Bill Walsh, former San Francisco 49ers coach,
Stanford University football coach

---

12. *No outlawing of high school letter jackets or T-shirts.*
32. *No dress code.*

In Sports

When John arrived at Saint John's, it was the rule "all over the land," he says, that the athletes didn't wear the high school letter jackets on campus. John changed that quickly. "I said to my players, 'The guy won it legitimately in a sport like football. He's proud of it. It's not going to hurt us to have him wear it. We want them to be proud of being an athlete. And that's not going to hurt us.' "

John puts the focus on pride.

Once John had a championship team with four men "festooned with full beards." Twenty-five years ago, when long hair was the in thing on campuses and parents got freaked out by it, one of John's key players was wearing long hair, and it was driving his dad crazy. The dad called John. "God, why don't you get Mike to cut his hair?" John's response: "If Mike cut his hair on this campus, this day and age, he'd be an oddball here. He's gotta be responsible like the other students. We want our football players to be students. We call 'em student athletes. Let's not make 'em different than the rest of the student body."

John recalls when all the coaches wore suits. Even ties. "The basketball coaches still wear 'em. They're the only guys in the gymnasium with a tie on."

He notes that today, "Even the monks here, they don't even wear the habits anymore. Everybody's casual."

In the Workplace

Everybody's casual? Not quite. There are still many workplaces that ration casual dress to Fridays. That rule seems ridiculous. If employees can do their jobs well in casual wear on Fridays, why not also on Mondays through Thursdays?

For those who insist on strict, formal dress codes, I'm reminded of a teacher's lesson. The teacher put up several sheets of white paper in front of his students. On the center of each sheet was a single black spot. He asked his students what they saw before them. Without exception, they all responded, "Black dots." Not one student saw all the white space surrounding the dots.

People too often focus their attention and thoughts on the black dots instead of on all the white spaces. They focus on the strange hair, on the body jewelry, or on the skin color of a person, when, instead, there is always more to an individual than one or two "black dots."

What's behind the hang-ups about dress? I think of the entrepreneur who built a very successful nationwide business and who casually told others that he never hired any man whose shoes weren't shined. I think of the woman who called me, asking for some guidance, because her husband refused to allow the women in his office to wear "men's clothes"—pants and slacks.

Rigid dress codes put the focus on *appearance* when the coach and the team need to focus on *performance*.

Certainly, some workplaces need dress codes. Some workplaces need work-related guidelines. But I'm for broadening what is acceptable to wear at work. Until just a few years ago, I always wore the traditional men's uniform at work: suit, dress shirt, and tie. Then I noticed that one of the men in the office was wearing sports shirts. At first I was uncomfortable about it and thought of telling him that sports shirts were unacceptable. After a few days, though, my thinking changed to "If he can do it, why can't I?" Since then, I have usually worn sports shirts. And now, when I wear suits and ties, I enjoy them and do it because I really want to that day.

NOODLES™

Copyright © 2000 Employers of America. NOODLES is a trademark of Employers of America.

⊔$⌐ **Chapter 16** ⊔$⌐

No Harassment. Period.

⊔$⌐ I tell our football players . . . "The incoming freshmen are jittery the way it is. They're nervous. So you make sure that you make them comfortable. Introduce yourself to 'em. Get their names. We have a contest to see who gets . . . who learns the most names. Always a couple of guys are incredible.

—John Gagliardi

---

13. No hazing tolerated.

In Sports

When John Gagliardi arrived at Saint John's in 1953, it was the tradition that, for the first six weeks of the new school year, upperclassmen harassed the freshmen in a demeaning and sometimes physically harmful way. Even now, hazing persists on some campuses and in some sports.

It was normally the star athletes, football and basketball players especially, who led the hazing at Saint John's. And that disturbed John. He couldn't believe what he was seeing. "They had big paddles. I couldn't believe the monks would allow it." He confronted some of his players. "I told my football players, 'You do what you want. But I do what

> [$] A jerk is someone who never says "Thank you."
> Someone who never says, "How's your kid doing? I
> heard he was sick." Someone who slams the door or
> gets in a bad mood."
>
> —Beverly Kaye, co-author of *Love 'Em or Lose 'Em*

I want, too. You do this, you aren't playing on my team.
And that means I don't want a guy that beats the holy hell
out of somebody. We're going to play clean football. I
wouldn't think of doing that, hit a guy with a paddle, on
the football field.' "

Then he laid down what must be the only YES (or positive) rule for the Johnnies. "We're going to have one rule
here. Treat the other guy the way you want to be treated."
Nearly 50 years later, John recalls this and says, "And that's
the only rule we've got to this day."

In the Workplace

This NO is a no-brainer. Hazing and harassment in the
workplace are, in most instances, going to get workplace
leaders and employers in legal trouble.

Is it too much to ask that everyone in the workplace—
from the top exec to the newest entry-level employee—act
as an adult? Adult behavior focuses on personal growth and
achievement and on getting the job done well. Adult behavior doesn't have time for hazing and harassing others.

If that isn't appealing, then focus on the 1998 U.S.
Supreme Court rulings and the 1999 Equal Employment
Opportunity Commission (EEOC) guidelines on harass-

ment and discrimination. The federal law and rules now clearly tell employers: If you want a defense against charges of illegal harassment or discrimination . . . you must demonstrate that you actively prohibit harassing and discriminatory behavior.

This NO is simple: No harassing, no discriminating. Period.

NOODLES™

⎰$⎱ Chapter 17 ⎰$⎱

No Busy Work

⎰$⎱ Anna Rose runs her last cross-country meet on
Thursday. It's a whole new subculture that we've
entered with this running. What impresses me the most
is the support for ALL the runners—even the ones who
come in ten minutes after everyone else is done. *Really!*
It's a neat group of kids and the sport doesn't seem to
draw the obnoxious parents that we saw in the soccer
world when Elliott did that. We certainly don't see six-
year-old cheerleaders. Don't even see 16-year-old
cheerleaders!

> —A parent, commenting about her 14-year-old
> daughter's cross-country track experience

---

14. *No creating busy work. Eliminate the
    unnecessary.*
15. *No changing our belief we must eliminate the
    unnecessary.*
87. *No precision pre-game drills.*
88. *No precision huddles.*
89. *No cheerleaders.*

In Sports

These NOs are the crux of John's contrarian system. No creating busy work. Eliminate the unnecessary. Eliminate frills

and time wasters, such as cheerleaders, precision huddles, and precision pre-game drills. Why? Because they have nothing to do with the team's one goal: winning the game.

Organized cheerleading was born in Minnesota (at the University of Minnesota in 1898), and it probably started its decline in Minnesota 55 years later, when Gagliardi arrived in Collegeville. "We think pep rallies are superficial," John says. "What do they have to do with anything? You've got to be prepared, know what you're doing. That's rally enough."

So out with the unnecessary. Focus on what leads to winning. Does precision in drills and huddles win a game? Then out with precision drills and precision huddles.

John once told an interviewer that watching his players come out of a huddle was like watching a kindergarten ballet class break up. So what. They win.

In the Workplace

Here's a good ongoing assignment for you and for everyone in your workplace. Eliminate your *cheerleaders*, your *precision drills*, and your *precision huddles*. Nearly every workplace has them and nearly everyone participates. They are the wasteful, profit-sucking, profit-killing *busy work* that most of us become comfortable with and become blind to.

Start with the cheerleaders. These are the people who eat up their own time and resources and who waste the time and resources of others. Years ago I shared an office suite with just such a cheerleader. Starting at about 9:30 each morning, he'd call around to the restaurants and cafes, asking about their luncheon specials. He spent much of the rest of the morning circulating around the suite, sharing the information with others and weighing his best choices for lunch. He was supposed to be out selling, but he contributed about as much to his employer as a cheerleader contributes to winning a game.

Reduce and eliminate the *cheerleading.*

Next, identify the precision drills and precision huddles. These are the activities and tasks you and others have always been doing just because "we've always done them that way." Or because they look good. Or because they make you feel good.

One way to identify the precision drills and precision huddles in your workplace is to send a memo to each person. At the top of it, write this question and request: "What are you regularly doing in your work that you believe you could stop doing and no one would notice, care about, or be harmed by? Write your answers on this sheet and return it to me by tomorrow noon." Thank everyone for answers and respond to their answers quickly.

NOODLES™

Copyright © 1995 Employers of America. NOODLES is a trademark of Employers of America.

⎣$⎦ **Chapter 18** ⎣$⎦

No Distractions from the Basics

⎣$⎦ You want to get it down to the basics with things
people love to have so you can do each item really,
really well. Be brilliant in the basics.

—Joe R. Lee, CEO, Darden Restaurants, Orlando, Florida

---

*16. No faltering in preparing to being brilliant in
the basics.*
*17. No lack of attention to fundamentals and the
little things.*

In Sports

Out with the unnecessary. In with the basics, the fundamentals.

"Football is a game of mistakes," John explains. "It's
just a game of mistakes and somehow you've got to eliminate 'em." Four things go into winning (not losing) a football game: (1) being brilliant in the basics, (2) making fewer
mistakes than the opposing team, (3) inviting fewer penalties than the opposing team, and (4) suffering fewer offici-
ating mistakes from the refs than the opposing team does.

John and his players can't do anything about refs who make lousy calls. But they can focus on the fundamentals—make fewer mistakes and give the refs fewer reasons to call penalties.

So, in Saint John's football, all the focus is on the fundamentals.

It's really simple, John says: "We lose when we make more vital mistakes than the opposition."

In the Workplace

Do you even know what the basics are in your position and in your company or organization? Do all the employees know what their basics are? What are the essential things you must do day-in, day-out, so that you and your company or organization win?

Everyone does these kinds of activities in the workplace: essential and profitable, essential and *un*profitable, and *un*essential and *un*profitable. An essential and profitable activity is anything you do that helps make a profit. You want to spend as much time as you can on these. An example of an essential and *un*profitable activity is completing tax records—it's essential to do but doesn't contribute to profits. You want to spend as little time on these as possible. An example of an *un*essential and *un*profitable activity is surfing the web while on work time, checking out personal sites and entertainment sites. You want to cut out the *un*essential and *un*profitable activities.

And the way to maximize the essential and profitable, reduce the essential and *un*profitable, and cut the *un*essential and *un*profitable is to focus on the basics and the little things. An excellent model is Boardroom, Inc., Greenwich, Connecticut, publisher of *Bottom Line/Business* and *Bottom*

Line/Personal. Marty Edelston, president, launched an "I Power" system in his workplace. He expects each employee to submit two suggestions a week. An example of how one employee focused on a little thing: The employee suggested making books one-eighth inch shorter to cut mailing costs. In the first year after implementing the idea, Boardroom saved more than $500,000.

That's being brilliant focusing on the basics!

⌊$⌋ Chapter 19 ⌊$⌋

No Substituting Mission Statements for Doing the Job

> ⌊$⌋ Get rid of company mission statements and core values. . . . They are actually quite destructive in that they create boxes that inhibit creativity, thwart agility, and defy change.
>
> —John R. Graham, Graham Communications, Quincy, Massachusetts

18. *No goals needed. We just expect great things to happen.*
20. *No "Mission Statement." Just win.*
107. *No promises. Just results.*

In Sports

Just as John says no to cheerleaders and precision drills, he's pretty sparse on goals, promises, and mission statements. Just as he has a disdain for the unnecessary, he has no time for goals and mission statements. Instead, John has an intense, deeply rooted focus on expecting to win, expecting great things to happen. "We really don't have any goals," he asserts. "I just believe in doing your best every day."

Again and again, John talks with his players about the Saint John's tradition of winning. His talks go something like this: "We have a great tradition. But what is tradition? It's only the fact that people like you have done great things before. All you have to do is continue to do those things, and it doesn't take a Superman to do these things." Then he may tell his players, "I'm just an ordinary guy that does ordinary things extraordinarily well. Running is an ordinary thing. An ordinary guy does it. But, the great runner is going to do it so well they make people avoid 'em."

As for goals, John says, "Try to make it simple. Never try to expose a team to so many goals or so many innovations that they lose track of the prime fact." And what's the prime fact for the Saint John's football team? "They are a good football team to begin with and they have nothing to fear."

In the Workplace

Whenever I hear or read the statement that every business and organization needs a mission statement and a vision statement, I wonder how humans, families, and nations made it into the 21st century *without* them.

I've written mission and vision statements for Employers of America. But I've never been pleased with them. Employees don't care for them. The statements never encompass all we can do or all we want to do. And what we do keeps changing. If no one pays attention to them, why waste time on them?

Nearly every mission and every vision statement I've ever read is as meaningless as the following gibberish, from a major-sized CPA firm: "We partner [Why did someone have to make a perfectly good noun into a verb?] with our clients to achieve their strategic business objectives through innovative solutions that align processes, people and technology." It's not quite as obtuse and ethereal as the following mission statement from a leading publisher and distributor of educational and training programs: "_____ will draw upon the most current base of knowledge, existing and emerging technologies, and all of the instructional and pedagogical resources available to develop and distribute instructional programs for education and training." Sure. Someone asks an employee of this firm what the company does and gets this answer: "We're in the *pedagogical* business."

Mission and vision statements are examples of *un*essential and *un*profitable activities.

What to do? Get everyone in your workplace focusing on helping make great things happen.

"Just win" is John's mission statement, though he doesn't call it that. When he says, "No 'Mission Statement,' " he's really saying no long-winded declaration that hangs on the wall and that everyone ignores. So what's a picture, in two or three words, that you and all of your people can focus your winning efforts on?

How about Make Great Things Happen?

⌊$⌋ **Chapter 20** ⌊$⌋

No Waiting for Luck

⌊$⌋ I learned that the most effective way to forge a
winning team is to call on the players' need to connect
with something larger than themselves.

—Phil Jackson, Chicago Bulls former coach,
Los Angeles Lakers coach

19. *No depending on good luck. Only bad luck can
    hinder us.*
21. *No problems or obstacles can stop us.*
34. *No superstitions.*

In Sports

The only good luck or bad luck in a football game is in an
official's call. Actually, John doesn't think of a wrong call as
bad luck so much as just "a *lousy* call." He grins when he
says, "We hope that they make it on the other team and not
on us."

But superstitions and bad luck don't stymie John's
teams. "We tell our men, 'We can overcome everything.'
We've got to have believers. We tell our guys, 'Winning is
going to take three things. Number one, you'd better play
the game of your lives, the best game you're capable of

$| It's no surprise that optimistic athletes, managers and
teams do better. What's interesting is where they do
better. It's in coming back from defeat and acting in the
clutch. For instance, optimistic swimmers often give
their best performances after having lost a race. In the
NBA, teams with high optimism are more likely to beat
the point spread in a game when they're coming off a
defeat.

—Martin Seligman, in a *Los Angeles Times* interview

---

playing. Number two, for the other team to beat us, we've got to screw up a lot. But those two won't beat us. The third thing, we have to have a monumental break from the officials.' " John adds, "In every game that we've lost we can point that out."

So no superstitions, no depending on luck to win. "We want our guys to be confident, but not arrogant," John explains. "We're trying to breed confidence. What we're really saying is, 'We expect to win.' "

John lumps belief in luck and superstitions with fear and says, "I don't preach out of fear, I coach out of preparedness. . . . If we are not playing up to our potential and if we make even a few mistakes we are vulnerable because of ourselves, not because of our rivals."

Talking about this, John laughs. "The only superstition I've got is, if we haven't got one more point than the other team has we're in trouble."

In the Workplace

About 20 years ago, I was teaching a *Start on Success* course for women wanting to launch their own businesses. I invited a friend, Cheryl Plagge, who owns a Management Recruiters franchise, to speak to the class. One of the women asked Cheryl how much luck had to do with her success. None, Cheryl answered, "Luck is preparation meeting opportunity."

Unfortunately, many people believe that success and winning depend on good luck, or that they are thwarted by bad luck. The lottery-gambling culture that's grown to permeate our society in the past 25 years must be conditioning a lot of people to believe that success and winning are all about luck.

One of my very successful employees links her daily successes to all kinds of superstitions. One day her success is because the Minnesota Vikings won the day before. If she's having a bad day, it's because the Vikings lost the day before. On another day, her success is because she's drinking Mountain Dew. I've not been able to convince her that her success is because she's skilled and persistent at what she does.

In our jobs and in our careers, we make our own luck. Sure, outside circumstances, competitors, and the economy (like lousy calls by sports officials) can roadblock us, sideline us, or set us back. But none of these will stop us when we forge ahead, focusing on making our own luck happen.

⌊$⌋ Chapter 21 ⌊$⌋

No Winning Without Fun

⌊$⌋ We've just held to our vision of making this work and having fun doing it.

> —Jim Lueders, co-owner, Sticks, Inc., Des Moines, Iowa,
> manufacturer of wood furniture

---

23. *No surviving without plenty of humor.*

In Sports

Saint John's University is a Benedictine school, founded and operated by Benedictine monks living the order's tradition of *Ora et Labora*, Latin for prayer and work. Most new students and faculty members at Saint John's quickly apply themselves to those tasks, studying, working, and praying. (Well, praying at least a little.) John Gagliardi, though, has put a twist on the university's culture. In coaching, and with his teams, it seems to be *play* and work.

"I don't think I could have lasted without humor," John explains. "Let's put it this way, there would have been no hope for me to have lasted without humor. Football is made for humor. You have to have a grin now and then on the gridiron. This isn't life and death."

The team practices usually begin and end with fun and some humor. Opening calisthenics (if you can call them that) might be *one* jumping jack and a Beautiful Day exercise (also called a Nice Day exercise), as described in Chapter 30. And the day's drills might end with half a dozen fun plays.

"Lord, if the game can't be fun, we shouldn't be playing it," John laughs.

In the Workplace

My son, David, who heads up the computer programming department for McLeod Publishing (a division of the communications firm McLeod USA), told me of hiring a woman who left a better-paying job to work for McLeod Publishing. I asked him what caused her to switch and take a cut in pay. She told him, "We were always too busy, too many projects at once. We had no time to have fun."

I know I couldn't have survived more than 50 years in the work world if I had not been able to see humor in some of the most disappointing and even desperate turns of events. And I've learned that people at work can inject humor into so many different situations.

One of my favorite office humor stories involved Brian, our development director, and Kim, who at the time was in charge of shipping. I had suggested that Kim research packing materials and costs and recommend the best solution. In a short time, Kim identified and received a sample bubble wrap. She was confident this plastic wrap, with tiny, air-filled bubbles, was the most cost-efficient answer. I heard her presenting the facts to Brian. Brian wasn't accepting her findings. Kim was getting exasperated—the numbers were so obvious. Finally, with a straight face and firm voice, Brian admonished Kim: "But Kim, you haven't added in the cost of blowing air into each bubble."

We end our employee handbook for our workplace with a few paragraphs about the importance of making a profit. It's headed "Profit Is Not a Dirty Word." But these are followed with this brief statement about fun:

> Fun isn't a dirty word, either. Many of the guidelines in this Handbook may seem kind of dull and serious. Still there is more to working here than the serious stuff. Let's have some fun, too. Share a joke, now and then, with others in the workplace. Share a cartoon. (Keep them clean, and nothing that's offensive.) Something funny happening in your life or family? Share it. Have an idea for a celebration now and then? Share it. Something good happening in your life? Share it.
>
> When you have a reason to be happy, pass it on. When you feel you *need* a reason to be happy . . . take a moment to look in a mirror . . . and smile.

Chapter 22

No Withholding Honor Earned

> I not only use all the brains I have, but all that I can borrow.
>
> —Woodrow Wilson

---

24. *No traditional captains. All seniors rotate this honor.*

94. *No guest speaker for football banquet. Seniors do the honor.*

In Sports

In NO #24 is some of John's humor. When he first explained this NO to me, he said, "It's so all the seniors can put on their resumés that they were captain of the football team."

But there are at least two other reasons for using all the seniors as captains and having seniors do the speaking at the annual football banquet. John knows that seniors have the experience to take on the responsibilities of leading the team. His whole coaching approach trains these young men for leadership. But even more important, he knows his

---

[$] A coach brings his or her team together, sometimes
every day, to discuss problems and strategy, boost
morale and listen to suggestions. Everybody has a voice.
Communication is constant. There's a lot of caring
going on . . . finding out where people are hurting,
counseling them, giving them a boost and assurances. A
good coach doesn't have team members who just want
to do a good job . . . they want to exceed the coach's
expectations.

Business practice tends to place power in the hands
of individual managers rather than in teams. But the
coach's very reason for existence is to enable the
transfer of power, authority and achievement to the
team.

—Ray Pelletier, president, The Pelletier Group

---

seniors are outstanding and accomplished and deserve the
opportunity to shine.

John is candid: "Most of my players . . . hell, they're
smarter than I am. I listen to them. I hope I'm teaching the
Johnnies to think for themselves."

In the Workplace

Once you pay people close to what they believe they are
entitled to make, the most powerful external motivator is
recognition. Don't dismiss the importance of titles. Sure,
some businesses and organizations are doing away with
titles. Everyone in these workplaces is an associate or some
such thing. But most people today still value titles. People
want their family and friends to know they are "captains"
of something.

Every employee has the potential to contribute something of value to your workplace. And every employee
wants some recognition.

At Employers of America, we have had telephone sales-people on our staff for most of the past 20 years. The near-universal title for these employees is *telemarketer, telephone service representative,* or *TSR.* Really makes them proud, right? Actually, they despise being called telemarketers. Our people do business-to-business calling. We call them *business sales consultants* (because that's the title they've asked for) and they're proud of their successes.

Patrick Lennahan, director of the Career Center at Roger Williams University, Bristol, Rhode Island, claims many people will take a prestigious title over more money. Jack Roseman, who boasts several titles, including associate director of the Donald H. Jones Center for Entrepreneur-ship, in the early 1970s saved his company several thou-sand dollars a year by offering his sales reps a choice: the title salesman or sales manager. The sales manager title came with about $2,000 less in annual income. Nearly all his sales reps picked the title manager with less pay.

NOODLES™

$\lfloor$ $\$$ $\rfloor$ **Chapter 23** $\lfloor$ $\$$ $\rfloor$

No Overdoing the Rules

$\lfloor$ $\$$ $\rfloor$ Curlers play to win but never to humble their opponents. A true curler would rather lose than win unfairly.

—From "Etiquette and Safety," a publication of the U.S. Curling Association

---

25. *No rules except the Golden Rule.*
26. *No one wanted except those who don't need rules. Those who need rules won't keep them.*
27. *No one wanted except those who do the right thing. We will surround them with others just like them.*

In Sports

The Pony of the Americas (POA) association has this motto: "Try hard, win humbly, lose gracefully and, if you must . . . protest with dignity."

That about sums up John Gagliardi's approach to coaching winning football teams. Well, all except that "protest with dignity" part. When John protests, it can be with a bit more than dignity.

But John and his teams do, very much and very often, win humbly.

How is it possible? Part of the answer must be no rules except the Golden Rule.

John learned his work ethic from his dad, a miner, a blacksmith, a body shop man. John learned to work in the body shop. He learned that "work can be fun, and fun can be work." No surprise, then, that an Associated Press reporter wrote that John's "philosophy is simple: Know your job and do it."

In the Workplace

Unfortunately, in today's work world, rules are needed. For example, the U.S. Supreme Court and the Equal Employment Opportunity Commission (EEOC) tell employers that they must have detailed, written rules outlawing harassment and discrimination.

But the spirit of John's "no rules except the Golden Rule" certainly is needed in the workplace. In fact, all the other rules an employer lays out, including the rules against harassment and discrimination, are meaningless and ineffective unless the spirit of the Golden Rule motivates the conduct of everyone in the workplace.

At Employers of America, we have a pretty detailed, specific set of workplace policies. And long ago I learned the truth of the second half of NO #26: "Those who need rules won't keep them."

Workplace leaders do need to set the example and demonstrate the spirit of the Golden Rule. Several years ago, I asked several of our employees to write an ethics policy for our employee handbook. What they drafted includes these words:

> One reason our association exists is to help each person in our workforce gain satisfaction from work accomplished here, and to grow in knowledge and skill. To succeed in this means there must be a spirit of trust between all of us in this workplace. The only way to establish and continue this trust is for each of us to speak and act honestly, legally, fairly, and ethically. We expect you to follow the Golden Rule when performing your work-related duties and in all your work-related activities and contacts. In other words, Do to others as you would have them do to you. Be fair, honest, and ethical. Deal with co-workers and members cheerfully and with respect.

NOODLES™

⌊$⌋ **Chapter 24** ⌊$⌋

No Time-Wasting Meetings

⌊$⌋ If you don't behave in a contrarian and counterintuitive way, you will only ever be moderately successful.

— Felix Dennis, chairman, Dennis Holdings Ltd.

---

28. No staff meetings.
29. No player meetings.
92. No off-season meetings.

In Sports

John is a minimalist. He focuses his mind and energies on those things that will assure that the team wins. He focuses the players on doing those things that increase their chances of winning. Thus, no formal meetings. At first he had no staff to meet with. Now, with a staff of four, he explains, "We have different duties. So I'll talk to one guy about his duties. Then another guy. Why get 'em all together?"

"I hate meetings, myself," he notes. "Most of them are a waste of time. So we don't want 'em." As for player meetings, "When school starts we never have any meetings except on Mondays. Instead of practice we look at video tapes."

Besides, what would John do at a player meeting? He's not much for pep talks and is as direct as an on-target forward pass. After the last practice on Friday, before a Saturday game, he'll remind the players of the basic game plan, tell them to conjure up all their plays working to perfection, picture their plays working with precision and perfection. He'll ask them to see themselves winning, exploding off the line of scrimmage, but always in control.

The Saint John's team needs no more meeting than that.

In the Workplace

Okay, we have to have some meetings at work. But nearly all of us really agree with John Gagliardi's "I hate meetings, myself."

Most meetings are painful wastes of time. Our culture seems cursed with meetings. And now the electronic media—under the fraudulent claim of saving us time—are making it possible for us to waste even more time in virtual meetings and slinging e-mail drivel back and forth.

Years ago, when I was a journalist covering school board meetings, I discovered two principles of meetings. The first is that, the more trivial the topic, the longer the discussion in the meeting. The second is that, the length of time a meeting will last is the number of participants multiplied by 15 minutes. If 10 people are present in a meeting, the meeting usually will last about 150 minutes (2 1/2 hours).

Little wonder that we hate meetings.

What to do?

At Employers of America, nearly all of our meetings are *stand-up* meetings. We tell our employees that anyone can call a stand-up meeting, with the people needed, on any topic that needs the people present. Several times a week, we'll hear someone call out, "Stand-up meeting, stand-up meeting."

The value of this? When people are standing, they think more clearly, and they want to talk less. The average length of a stand-up meeting in our workplace? The number of people present multiplied by one to three minutes.

NOODLES™

Copyright © 1993 Employers of America. NOODLES is a trademark of Employers of America.

⌊$⌋ **Chapter 25** ⌊$⌋

No Put Downs

⌊$⌋ It's up to us to prevent the violence. It's up to us to treat people with respect so they don't feel bad about themselves.

—Sam McGrane, student, Riceville, Iowa, High School

33. *No nicknames unless complimentary.*

In Sports

"Ever notice that most nicknames aren't complimentary?" John asks. He wants no negatives corrupting the mettle of his winning teams. So nicknames are out, unless complimentary.

In the Workplace

Keep negative, insulting, put-down names out of your workplace. They can create or lead to a harassing and discriminatory atmosphere, which can lead to legal trouble. Who needs that?

More important, there's real value in positive, uplifting, complimentary names. People live down to their names or they live up to their names. Ask your employees the names or nicknames they prefer, and use the names they prefer. It's the Golden Rule in practice.

NOODLES™

⌊$⌋ Chapter 26 ⌊$⌋

No Substituting Reams
of Paper for Action

⌊$⌋ It appears that America's work ethic is changing from
working hard to working smart.

> —Sharon Leonard, manager of workplace trends and
> forecasting, SHRM, in *HR Magazine*

35. No playbooks.
73. No scripted plays.
74. No print handouts given to players.

In Sports

Why no playbooks? Because players don't read them. "This
No throws everybody," John notes. "Our defense has none.
Nothing. But we only led the nation on defense just a cou-
ple years ago. We led the nation!"

John's players get what they need. The tight end gets
one page of blocking rules. That's his playbook. Each position gets one page. The backs and linemen might get three
pages. "Most of the time we don't even give 'em that, they
just learn 'em on the field," John explains. "We think you
have to learn it on the field."

It works, too. "We were eleven and 0 before we lost a heartbreaker, in the playoffs," John says. "And we set the all-time scoring record. I don't think it will ever be broken."

In the Workplace

Job descriptions are kind of like playbooks. Employees seldom read them. The same with employee handbooks. Job descriptions and handbooks are important in most workplaces, not because employees read and internalize them but because they're helpful tools the manager and the employee can use from time to time.

On the job daily, though, what matters isn't what's on paper in the job description or in the handbook. What matters for success and high achievement is learning the job—starting on day one—"on the field." What matters is the coaching and the experience the employee gets, not what's on paper

⌊$⌋ **Chapter 27** ⌊$⌋

No Playing Favorites

⌊$⌋ . . . Singling out top performers can actually hasten
their departure while alienating other people.

—*Harvard Management Update*, August 1999

36. *No statistics posted.*
37. *No newspaper clippings posted, ours or theirs.*
47. *No posting anything on bulletin board except
    travel information and kicking teams.*
70. *No "Big" game we point to.*
86. *No counting tackles. We play a team defense.*

In Sports

No statistics posted, no newspaper stories posted, no star
players spotlighted. For a number of reasons.

First, John tells his players that nothing is older than
yesterday's headlines, win or lose. The only thing that matters is this week's game.

Second, John says posting statistics isn't important.
"Our players know what we're doing. But we don't want
anything individual put up. We just figure we're just going

|$| Instead of always giving the "high five" to the running
|T| back, let's every now and then give thanks to the
teammates who helped make possible the run, the
score, and the visible achievement.

—Dave Worman, author of *Motivating Without Money*

---

to do it [win] again! What you've done is done. Now you've got to do it again. You've got to line up and do it again next Saturday. Don't get side-tracked and dwell too much on the past."

Third, this is a team sport. "The guy who makes a tackle isn't necessarily the one to get all the credit. Because the other 10 guys might have done their job very well and forced the play. It's a team defense with us," John explains. "Same with the quarterback who throws the ball and makes a completion. Whether the guy who threw that ball or the guy who catches it, the linemen had to do their jobs. That's a team deal."

In the Workplace

No playing favorites if you want all the people in your workplace working together as a team. This doesn't mean you don't recognize individual success and individual contributions. Even though people today, more than ever before, work on teams, individuals still want and need personal attention.

Years ago one of my key assistants, whose office was right next to mine, told me that one of the employees said to her, "Jim always says `Good morning' to you but never to me." My assistant suggested I make a point of greeting everyone each morning. So I did, and continue to do it. Until one morning about three months ago. I came in to work with things preoccupying my mind a bit more than usual. I did greet nearly everyone. But then about 10 A.M., Penny, who works at the other end of the suite from me, stopped at my door and said, "You didn't say 'Good morning' to me."

This is the key: When a success is a team's success, recognize everyone who shares in the success.

NOODLES™

⌊$⌋ **Chapter 28** ⌊$⌋

No Shirking Responsibility

⌊$⌋ It's your choice, your life. A lot of people want to blame things on others or on how they grew up and not look at themselves. But at some point you have to be responsible for what you do.

—Marcus Robinson, Chicago Bears wide receiver

38. *No excuses.*
39. *No denying responsibility for own actions.*
40. *No blaming anyone else for your or their mistakes.*

In Sports

"That's important. No excuses at all. Because then you don't accept responsibility," John says.

His focus is on personal responsibility, on shouldering it.

"That's the only way you can coach people," he says. "Because if they don't acknowledge a mistake, they're doomed to repeat it. You don't dwell on it. But the coach has to point out the error. But do it in a way that doesn't destroy the guy. He's got to realize what he did and then try to avoid it. The longer I coach the more I'm into this."

|$| Developing a positive attitude towards safe
 T   [motorcycle] riding is not easy. It means saying "no" to
     dangerous behavior that gives a rider maximum thrill. It
     means saying "no" to peer pressure. Saying "no" to the
     desire to show off.

—James K. Kelly, nationally certified motorcycle
safety instructor, motorcycling columnist

In the Workplace

It's no surprise that the *Christian Science Monitor* (Aug. 20, 1999) quotes Caroline Forell, a University of Oregon law professor: "There's this belief among Americans that, if I'm injured, someone has to be at fault."

How does this work in your workplace? An employee who has a real or perceived grievance can begin to sulk and quickly can feel a victim. Then this employee begins to contemplate which law (or perceived legal protection) can bring a quick redress. Lest you think I'm paranoid, let me insert a disclaimer here. Most employees are great people. They do their very best, and do it well. And I wouldn't repeal any of the civil rights laws or the other laws that give employees protections in the workplace.

That said, as we begin the 21st century, there appears to be a great chance that you will have more headaches from employee-caused legal actions than you might suffer losses and headaches from fire, tornadoes, theft, and embezzlement combined.

Several years ago, *Forbes* had a story headed "Boss Harassment." Included was this statement: "Employers are in the same position that doctors found themselves in during the '70s and '80s."

$\lfloor$ \$ $\rfloor$ There can be no excuses. You can't say that you didn't
$\top$ like the snow or that you didn't feel up to top form.

—Jean-Claude Killy, skier, three-time Olympic gold medalist

So what do you do? How do you develop a team of employees who eagerly accept responsibilities? You have to have what I call an adult-to-adult workplace culture. An adult-adult relationship means you act as an adult in your dealings with employees. You do your best to be objective, not emotional, and fair. And it means you expect—and require—your employees to act as adults.

Here are seven ways to help your employees accept their responsibilities and improve their performance:

1. Adopt adult policies for dealing with your employees. Adult policies are fair and clearly stated. And adult policies are consistently and fairly applied.
2. Use hiring procedures that result in hiring qualified people who will work together in your culture.
3. Orient and train your people in a coaching way, not in a dictating parent way. Train by showing. Train by letting new employees fail without criticism, by giving them time to succeed. Train by praising success.
4. Use a *performance objective* evaluation system to encourage your employees to perform better. With your employee, identify the performance you and the employee want. Decide on the time frame for achievement. Agree on the training and coaching you will give the employee. Evaluate the achievement of goals in a timely way. Confer with the employee regularly.

5. Set up a pay-benefit package you can afford. Tie it to the performance you want or to the goal you want to achieve.

6. Regularly communicate what you want. Communicate to your employees how their efforts are contributing to the success of your business or organization.

7. Discipline and terminate fairly.

There are excuses and explanations, and there is commitment. I don't want excuses and I don't care for explanations. What I want from employees and associates are explanations *with* commitment to get the job done right.

NOODLES™

Copyright © 1997 Employers of America. NOODLES is a trademark of Employers of America.

⌊$⌋ Chapter 29 ⌊$⌋

No Being a Jerk

⌊$⌋ I've definitely got to tone down my antics a little bit. I've got to let my play speak louder than my extracurricular activities on the court.

—Jacob Jaacks, University of Iowa
Hawkeye basketball center (1999)

---

41. No tolerating loud-mouths, braggarts, or show-offs.

In Sports

John's focus is on the *team's* winning. He knows that great players think first about the team. He tells aspiring coaches: "Every team has loud-mouths. Every team has braggarts. Most teams harbor jealousy. You have to snuff it out at the beginning."

"Through the years I've noticed that the greatest, the better the ball player, the nicer the guy," John says. "The less arrogant he is." John tells his new players, "Think about the best player on your high school team. Was he a nice guy? Or was he a big jerk?" John tolerates no jerks!

Then John comments on that enshrined sports code: Nice guys finish last. He says, "Maybe, maybe some do. But a lot of nice guys finish first. And a lot of lousy guys finish last. They're in prison, and they're everywhere else in the world."

Kind of strange, isn't it, an exceptionally successful college coach using the words "be nice"? John tells players, "Believe you can be a nice guy and be an athlete." What a contrast to the almost daily headlines in sports sections about trashy, braggart, even criminal athletes.

In the Workplace

I'm reminded of the response of an attendee in one of my workshops for employers. I'd covered many of the legal obligations employers have involving their employees and was going beyond that to discuss the importance of employers, managers, and supervisors being *fair* with their employees. A business owner, seated in the back row, interrupted me with a statement, more than a question: "As long as I'm legal, why do I have to be fair?"

The answer is simply this. People want to be treated fairly. People want to work with and work around others who are—yes—nice. A friend told me she had finally quit her job at a local retail store. I was surprised. I'd thought she had enjoyed her work. "What caused you to quit?" I asked. "I just can't stand being around negative people," she said. "And just about everyone in that store is negative."

I'm reminded, too, of a Guaymi (a Central American Indian) dawn song's guidance from The Great One, the

Lord of the Dawning. It's good advice to all of us who coach and lead: "Be kind, be kind, be brave, be brave, be pure, be pure, be humble as the earth, and be as radiant as the sunlight!"

NOODLES™

⌊$⌋ **Chapter 30** ⌊$⌋

No Being a Drill Sergeant

⌊$⌋ In the Navajo way, we rise with the sun. We get up early, around 5 or 5:30, and give thanks for the day. We think nothing but good thoughts during the day.

> —Ira Vandever, Drake University (Des Moines, Iowa) quarterback, describing how his Navajo upbringing gives him strength, a sense of purpose

---

42. *No resemblance to a BOOT CAMP.*
49. *No agility drills.*
50. *No lengthy calisthenics (about four minutes of stretching).*
51. *No calisthenics when Daylight Savings time ends. Darkness limits practice to 30 minutes.*
52. *No pre-practice drills. Players are on their own.*
58. *No laps.*
59. *No wind sprints.*
60. *No yelling or screaming at players.*
61. *No getting in player's face.*
62. *No water or rest denied when players want it.*
65. *No underclassmen carry equipment other than their own.*

> $ | It's time to do away with coaching by humiliation and
> fear. When college coaches choose to coach this way
> and win, then coaches at all levels feel they have to
> emulate this behavior. This results in an environment
> with an enormous rippling effect with harmful social
> consequences. . . . As parents and citizens, we must
> stop honoring this primitive and abusive behavior that
> is tolerated and perpetuated in the name of "winning."
>
> —Bill Reichardt, former football player with the
> University of Iowa and the Green Bay Packers

67. *No practice outside in rain, excessive heat, cold,
    or threat of lightning.*
68. *No practice outside if mosquitoes or gnats
    are bad.*

In Sports

This is the big one. This one—NO #42—and the related
NOs are what really set John Gagliardi's coaching apart
from traditional coaching.

The Saint John's team turns drills and calisthenics into
comedy. Opening calisthenics might be one—yes, one—
jumping jack. Next might be a Nice Day drill. There's that
nice word again. It's also called the Beautiful Day drill.
Here's how it's done on a crisp, blue-sky fall afternoon, on
the field surrounded by oak, elm, birch, and towering pine
trees on the Saint John's campus. In football practice gear,
the young men drop to the ground, lie there on their backs,
and stretch out on the field. They stare up at the relaxing
blue Minnesota sky and take in the warmth of the fall sun
for a few minutes. And they turn their heads to players next

> [$|T] John Gagliardi is speaking to a business audience, and he's asked why he doesn't believe in traditional calisthenics. He says, "A kid goes out to play kick-the-can. He doesn't do calisthenics first. In a rout some guys wait 'til near the end of the game to go in. So we do calisthenics before the game and the guy sits a couple hours. What good's the calisthenics done him?"

to them and greet each other with an enthusiastic, "NICE DAY!" or "BEAUTIFUL DAY!"

Nothing mean. No drill sergeant coach or coaching assistants screaming at them.

It's as if John pampers the men! No practice in the rain, in excessive heat, in excessive cold. No practice outside when the mosquitoes or gnats are bad. (You've got to experience fall in Minnesota lake country, amid the pines, to appreciate this NO.) And you have to appreciate John. "We don't have to get wet unnecessarily, 'cause it isn't going to do any damn good." So the team goes inside to practice.

John's approach is common sense, trust, the coaching of a gentleman. No getting in a player's face. No water or rest denied. He tells his players: "Whenever you need water, just go, it's always available, go get it. If you think you need a break, a breather, you don't need permission, we trust you. We know you're not going to loaf."

Meanness, agility drills, and lengthy calisthenics are supposed to toughen up the young men in sports, toughen them to endure through the tough games. But John early on figured out a secret to the game. It isn't boot camp conditioning that prepares winners. It isn't meanness, toughness, and endurance that win the games. Years ago John figured out

---

⌐$⌐ What the mind believes, the body achieves. That's why
ㅜ we train athletes and top performers to relax and
mentally picture their performances first before they go
out and do something. Since the mind doesn't know
the difference between a real and imagined event, the
nervous system will lay down neural images of the
performance you are envisioning. When a person
actually does perform, it's like *deja vu* all over again.

—Richard F. Gerson, president, Gerson
Goodson Performance Management

---

that football players move at full speed for only eight minutes
a game! An average of 160 plays at three seconds each. The
game is made up of quick, disciplined thrusts and bursts of
energy. It's skill, precision, and discipline that win the games.

In the Workplace

Far too many workplaces resemble not just boot camps,
but battlefields. Bosses are bossy and dictatorial. Employees behave as spoiled brats. The American culture is a vio-
lent and self-absorbed culture, and this violence and self-
ishness intrude into our workplaces, too. A human
resources consultant in Boise, Idaho, recently said managers spend as much as 20% of their time resolving
employee battles. And a study by the Saratoga Institute,
based on more than 20,000 exit interviews, found that poor
supervisor behavior was the main reason for people's quitting their jobs.

In the workplace, as in sports, there is coaching and
there is coaching. There is coaching that turns out arrogant loud-mouths. (I'm reminded of Dallas Cowboys
coach Jimmy Johnson, a few years ago, just before the

NFC title game against the 49ers, calling a Fort Worth radio program. He boasted: "We will win the ball game. And you can put it in three-inch headlines. We will win the ball game.") Try to imagine customers or clients saying, "We sure like Pete's cocky promises." Try to imagine employees saying, "We sure enjoy getting kicked around by the boss."

And there is coaching that turns employees, and players, into life-long winners.

Which kind of coach do you think your customers or clients want to do business with? Which kind of coaching will achieve the most with employees?

$|$ Chapter 31 $|$

No Focusing on Mistakes

> $|$ We want total concentration on the next opponent. We
> don't want to think about what we did last week.
>
> —John Gagliardi

43. *No compulsory film sessions except Monday*
(only day team looks at films).
71. *No grading films.*

In Sports

John uses film (video) sessions to reinforce all the other
things he and the players do to build confidence for the
next win. So no overuse of video sessions. One session, on
Monday, and that's mostly focused on what the players did
right in Saturday's game.

In pre-season sessions, he'll show videos of classic Johnnies victories and repeat to the players "that you can win
by doing a few ordinary things extraordinarily." He'll say,
"We're not going to show you the Vikings or Notre Dame,
we're going to show you Saint John's. We're not even going
to show you the national championship teams. We're going

to show you last year's team. We don't have to go way back. Just, some of you guys did this! And you new guys are going to have to do this. This is the way we want it done." And, he says, then the players visualize it.

Think of these video sessions as the coach's weekly performance reviews. "The beautiful part about video tape," John explains, "we can edit it and just show the successes that we had." He continues: "If any guy did anything that was very good, then we show that and then praise. Try to praise the heck out of him. If it's good enough everybody spontaneously applauds him."

Mistakes? Not shown when the team is together. Only when the men break into offensive and defensive. Then the offensive and the defensive coaches show them the mistakes. "We don't want them to be too tough, don't dwell on them, but point 'em out," John says. He pauses. "I'm not even so sure we should even do that part. If we just showed 'em what we really want them to do, how we want it done, and leave, I think I'd be happier with it."

In the Workplace

That's what feedback, appraisals, and job performance reviews should be like: Emphasize the positive. Most employees get little or no formal reviews, and most of the feedback they get from the boss is negative.

Far more valuable, far more effective for everyone's success, is emphasis on the positive. And that takes an approach entirely different from the traditional, formal, ogre-type appraisal. Think of feedback and appraisals as performance video sessions with the employee. Focus on what the employee has been doing right. Encourage the employee to do self-evaluation on where and in what ways the employee can improve performance. Then together agree on ways the employee, the supervisor, and the employer will make it possible for the employee to succeed.

NOODLES™

⎣$⎦ **Chapter 32** ⎣$⎦

No Substituting Putzing
for Achieving

⎣$⎦ Citing Parkinson's Law (work expands to fill the time
allowed for its completion), Ron Rowe, president and
CEO of J.W. Pepper & Sons, Inc., says: "It's true no
matter what you do and no matter what your job is."

—*Smart Workplace Practices* newsletter, February 1999

---

44. No practice on Sunday or Monday.
45. No long practices: 90 minutes Tuesday,
   Wednesday, Thursday; 30–45 minutes on Friday.
46. No practice schedule posted.
66. No spring practice.
93. No captains' practice.

In Sports

John pioneered the reduction of practicing six and seven
days a week. "They used to go seven days a week," he
notes. "We don't have any meetings, nothing, on Sundays.
And Mondays we don't practice." Years ago he cut spring
practice and long practices. He's cut practicing to the essentials in 30 to 90 minutes. "We think we're going to do all that
we have to do in that time, and why keep staying out there
when we're done? All you do is risk fatigue and injury."

John's players aren't practicing to build brute strength and Herculean endurance. His players are practicing to develop their skills and to apply their brainpower. John once explained it this way to a sports writer: "While the other team is putting muscle against muscle, we're putting brain power against brain power. At the end of the season our foes are becoming tired physically, which means tired thinking. They'll be accumulating bruises and ills and we will, hopefully, have accumulated mental toughness, with quick reactions and the ability to `read' the game."

In the Workplace

This is the key to getting what you want in your career, in your business or organization. To focus your brainpower on the essentials. To focus energies and resources on the essentials.

The productivity of American workers soared in the 1990s and continues to edge up. Still, I believe that most workers—from the top CEOs to the entry-level people—are wasting from 10% to 30% of their time and energies on nonessential and nonprofitable activities. Example today: computer putzing. Do all the data we enter into a computer really need to be there? Do we really need all the reports that we run? The more computer power we have and the more exotic the program, the more time we waste. Reid Goldsborough, author of *Straight Talk About the Information Superhighway*, writes this in *Smart Workplace Practices* newsletter: "When you take the time to note your own work habits and those of people around you, you begin to see some of the reasons why [PCs haven't had a positive impact on productivity]. . . . Those memos with their fancy fonts and elaborate formatting take longer to create than the simple typewritten memos of the past. Likewise with those slick presentations adorned with graphics, sound effects, and animation. E-mail makes it easy to stay in the loop, but wading through scores of nonessential messages a day is a time sink."

Nearly every one of us in our workplaces spends time "practicing" (putzing) when we could be producing.

We need shorter meetings.

We need to focus our time and energies.

We need to end our work before we become fatigued.

We need to use our brains more.

Our association's legal counsel, Dan Dudley, in Tucson, Arizona, miraculously recovered from the killer strep A disease. (It's the disease that killed Muppets creator Jim Henson.) Dan survived but lost both legs below the knee, his lower left arm and hand, most of the fingers on his right hand, and even the tip of his nose (his friends tell him that was an improvement). When I visited Dan in the hospital, as he was beginning his recovery, he was in bed and apologized to me. He told me one client already had removed him as his attorney, and Dan told me he would understand if I also wanted to get another attorney.

"I don't hire you for your feet," I assured him. "I hire you for your brain."

NOODLES™

Copyright © 2000 Employers of America. NOODLES is a trademark of Employers of America.

⌊$⌋ **Chapter 33** ⌊$⌋

No Unnecessary Anything

⌊$⌋ They're all human beings. They all have mothers. We don't like to hurt people, number one.

         —John Gagliardi, on why "No tackling" in practice

---

48. *No practice pants issued. Shorts or sweats worn at all practices.*
53. *No practice apparatus or gadgets.*
54. *No blocking sleds.*
55. *No blocking or tackling dummies.*
56. *No tackling.*
57. *No whistles.*
63. *No traditional drills.*
64. *No practice modules.*
69. *No practice under lights to get ready for an away night game.*
96. *No compulsory weight program.*

In Sports

No traditional anything. That's how all these NOs could be lumped together. But that's too sweeping. The better, more

$ | Some games take weeks, months, even years to play
   out, and that, incidentally, is why you generally have
more than one game at a time in progress—and some
that are more urgent and important than others. If a
play is not absolutely essential or won't pick up any
yardage, don't keep sending your players out for passes
just to keep the arm in shape. If you do, they will soon
get bored and possibly even ask to get out of their
contract. Meetings that are not necessary and phone
calls that don't really accomplish anything all fall into
this category. You can overdo "fire drills" to the point
that everybody's too tired to answer the bell when a
real fire breaks out.

> —Jerry Baker, America's master gardener,
> in *Jerry Baker's Growth Plan for People*

accurate NO here is "No doing anything that's a waste of time."

"We eliminate the unnecessary," John says. "And most of the things I find in coaching are unnecessary." He chuckles when he says this. "We've eliminated almost everything." He smiles when he says this. "We've cut to the important things more than anybody else in practices. So we actually spend more time practicing than others, practicing the necessary stuff."

Take "No practice under lights to get ready for an away night game." Saint John's doesn't have lights. No problem. John doesn't take the team to a field with lights to prepare for the night games. "We don't want to make the players think that it's going to matter. Besides, we're not going to be playing in the dark!"

"Put it this way," John says. "We're going to make things [in practice] as game-like as we can. . . . We're going to do everything we can to simulate the game date, except going to the ultimate step [tackling] and risk the injury."

In the Workplace

Question everything you do. And coach your employees to question the value and pay-off of everything they do. How many "traditional drills" do you and your employees do that are a waste of time and money?

Barry Schimel, a CPA and president of The Profit Advisors in Rockville, Maryland, tells of working with bank employees, encouraging them to identify unnecessary activities. Finally, hesitantly, several of the employees mentioned a certain report they spent a lot of their time regularly preparing for one of the managers. The manager was present in the session. He spoke up, with some disbelief, and said that he had never requested the report. He had no use for it.

In your work, focus on execution, not on activity. Move the ball; don't run laps. Too many people believe that talking, traveling, motion, data feeding, and data eating means the job is getting done. Usually, we know what has to be done. What we're really doing, much of the time, is substituting running laps for moving the ball.

I recall an inquiry I received from a project director with a large firm in the Detroit area. She was looking for the most successful suggestion program in the country. Could I give it to her? I explained that I had been examining many successful suggestion and employee involvement programs over the past 20 years and that there was no one best program. I explained that I could coach her and her people to design their own best program, one that brought out the best involvement in their own workplace.

Many of us waste a lot of time looking for the perfect strategy or perfect execution when we could be executing what we already know works well.

⚑ Chapter 34 ⚑

No Celebrating the Heroes Only

⚑ I learned in football that you shouldn't try to score on every play. Get the first downs and the touchdowns will hit you in the face.

—Jack Kemp, former NFL quarterback and U.S. congressman

---

75. No big deal when we score. We expect to score.

In Sports

Some odd chemistry, or perhaps just the corrupting influence of sports TV and extravagant journalism sports puffery, has caused an explosion of showing off. In football, the flamboyant craziness of strutting, jumping, and shouting after scoring has led to a rule against it in the end zone.

"All these great celebrations, they go crazy like scoring was some miracle," John observes. "We don't. We expect to score." He continues: "That doesn't mean you can't go over and tell a guy, `Nice job!' We do that." But no celebrating the heroes. "The linemen open a tremendous hole and one guy goes waltzing into the end zone. Now he's the big hero. But it was the linemen who put him in the end zone."

> ⬛$ It is far better to have people regard you with a sense of trust, rapport, and good will than a desire for revenge.
>
> —Tom Krattenmaker, author and director of news and information at Swarthmore College

When everyone on the team is working together and expecting to win, scoring by one person isn't such a big deal.

In the Workplace

"I think the superstars are going to have to play more like team players," Milwaukee Bucks coach George Karl told a pro basketball reporter after the NBA announced rule changes early in 2001, including allowing zone defenses. Bringing back zone defenses after more than 50 years is one way the NBA wants to de-emphasize stars and individual play and to put the emphasis on team play.

It's the same in the workplace. The *Harvard Management Update* (August 1999) wrote in a brief story headed "Should You Focus on Stars at All?": ". . . Some executives of low-turnover companies argue that a star system can be counterproductive. The reason: singling out top performers can actually hasten their departure while alienating other people." In the story Dave Russo, of SAS Institute, explains: "We

> ⬛$ To win consistently, you have to have people who are able to drop the "me first" ethic. . . . We have to have players who can be taught to subvert their own egos for the common good.
>
> —Arthur Resnick, physical education teacher and coach, Scarsdale High School, quoted in *Boardroom Reports*

⌊$⌉ The notion that the whole is greater than the sum of the parts must be an overriding principle for the team, so much so, that **no single player will ever be more important than the team.** . . . A team should always take time out to **celebrate little victories.**

—Robert Evangelista, in *The Business of Winning: A Manager's Guide to Building a Championship Team at Work*

have avoided anointing people as stars and fast-trackers, although we have people with star talent. It's not been our pattern to identify people as stars because we don't think that helps our organization." And Mike Croxson of Synovus Financial says: "I can't say, 'We're a high-potential company,' and then look at two people and say, 'You're high-potential and you're low potential.' Folks on the team aren't stupid. They see the disconnect."

NO #75 really is about banning exaggerated celebrations and pompous behavior by and for individual performance. It turns off most people in the workplace. No one cares to work around the blowhard or sit in the shadow of the superstars.

When you want *team* performance in your workplace, celebrate your *team's* successes.

⊔$⊔ Chapter 35 ⊔$⊔

No Pushing Unwanted Rewards

⊔$⊔ If you have a job without aggravations, you don't have a job.

—Malcolm Forbes

---

76. No Gatorade® celebrations.

In Sports

Definitely, no Gatorade® celebrations. Pouring bottled liquid all over a winning coach is juvenile and dumb.

"We don't tolerate that," John says. "I don't want to catch pneumonia. I tell 'em, 'God, it's not anything, didn't you expect us to win? How'd you like Gatorade® thrown on you?' It's gotten to be another stupid tradition. Asinine. Besides, I don't want to wreck my clothes, you know."

John recalls his first year coaching at Carroll College in Helena, Montana. "We won a big game and they want to throw me in the showers. I say to 'em, 'Anybody that touches me's off the team **right now!** What the hell you want to go throwing me in the shower? Do I get punished because we won the game? Why punish me?" He laughs, telling about it: "Why punish me?"

In the Workplace

Misplaced enthusiasm. Misdirected exuberance. Inconsiderate recognition. How easily leaders and their teams can cross the line from genuine, warm compliments to outright offensive behavior.

What's the right way to recognize the people we coach and supervise? For answers, I visited with Rosalind Jeffries, president of Performance Enhancement Group, a management training firm in Chevy Chase, Maryland, and author of *101 Recognition Secrets.* Jeffries cited her research showing that confident workers are more productive and creative. Her conclusions are based on responses from more than 10,000 managers and employees she has interviewed and taught over the past 17 years. Seven out of 10 people reported they want specific day-to-day recognition of their contributions at work. Not big, super, surprising celebrations. Recognition. Said Jeffries, "People are starved for attention."

But it has to be the right kind of attention, the right kind of recognition.

Jeffries told of the Christmas gift given by an all-white management to 300 employees (99% of whom were African American) in the nutrition department at a large medical center. Management gave these employees who work around food all day, all year long the gift of popcorn! "The employees rebelled," she said. "They thought, `Why not a $3 gift certificate for renting a video?' "

Next she told me of the manufacturing company president who did it all wrong. He intended to recognize and reward a line employee who had come up with an idea to save a ton of money. So the boss invited the guy and his wife to dinner at a high-class restaurant. "The guy told me it was the most uncomfortable evening he'd ever had," said

Jeffries. "The suit he was wearing was 10 years old and didn't fit. It cost him $200 because his wife had to buy a new dress. He didn't know what to talk about and he had three forks and didn't know what to do with them."

Jeffries asked the fellow what he would have liked the president to give him. He said, "To come down the line and thank me, and maybe give me a six-pack of beer."

Jeffries also cited good examples of the right kinds of recognition. There's the boss who gives a plant to an employee as a way to encourage the employee to grow in the job and says, "Watch it grow as you grow in new skills."

There's the boss who needs an employee, who is the mother of a young child, to come in to work overtime on a weekend. He buys a $1.99 child's puzzle and gives it to the employee and tells her to give it to her child and tell the child, "My boss thanks you for allowing Mom to work on the weekend and take time away from you."

The best (and yet inexpensive) form of recognition? "The most popular is the pat on the back, it's always number one," Jeffries said. "And a thank you is right at the top, too."

NOODLES™

⎣$⎦ Chapter 36 ⎣$⎦

No Trashy, Cheap Behavior

⎣$⎦ When you resort to trash talking to try to defeat
someone else, you are admitting that you can't beat
them using skills and play execution.

> —Richard Stratton, associate professor of health
> and physical education at Virginia Tech

---

77. *No trying to "kill" opponent.*
78. *No trash talk tolerated.*
84. *No cheap shots tolerated.*

In Sports

Sports violence goes back centuries. Wray Vamplew heads
the International Centre for Sports History and Culture at
De Montfort University in Leicester, England. In his book
Pay Up and Play the Game (a history of sports), he describes
sports violence throughout the centuries that makes Mike
Tyson look like a wimp. He agrees with late Chicago Cubs
manager Leo Durocher, who asserted that nice guys finish
last. Vamplew told Stephen Wade of the Associated Press,
"Personally, I can't see how people get to the top of sport
without trampling on other people and groups."

John Gagliardi vehemently insists it doesn't have to be
that way. And one by one, a few leaders in sports—from lit-

> $ I'd like to go back to the purposes of having intercollegiate and interscholastic sport with a theme of "And that's what sport should be all about." This approach necessitates reshaping the culture around sport: a culture that clearly demonstrates that the games are *not* for the glory of the coach or parents, but for the growth of the participants . . . a culture that teaches the young not to hate their opponents, but to honor them, since without opponents there would be no game—without *great* opponents they would never be challenged to perform at a higher level of play.
>
> —Christine H.B. Grant, University of Iowa women's athletic director

tle leagues to national pro leagues—are agreeing with him. Parents of youth sports playing in Los Angeles are asked to sign a promise of good behavior. In Jupiter, Florida, parents are required to take a good-sportsmanship class before their children can play ball.

John's lifelong record proves that a sports team can win by superior execution and by eliminating mistakes. "We're not trying to kill anybody," he explains. "We want to tackle, we want to get the job done, we want to block. We don't want to kill. . . . We don't get any extra points for that."

John recalls when a new player, just before a game, started boasting, "Oh, we're gonna kick ass." John pulled him over and told him, "We're just going to play this game. We're going to win. Kick ass? What does that mean? Don't tell me what you're going to do. Just go do it. That means win!"

In the Workplace

Killing in the workplace is real. Trash talk and cheap behavior at work can lead to harassment and discrimination charges against the supervisor and the employer, and they can trigger violence and ultimately killing. Sadly, workers are taking into the workplace the trash and violence they experience on the streets and view on television and at sports and entertainment events.

The U.S. Supreme Court and the Equal Employment Opportunity Commission (EEOC) have made it clear to supervisors and employers. If you want a defense against an employee's charge of illegal harassment or illegal discrimination, then you must have—and must enforce—a clear, detailed policy against all kinds of unwelcome harassing, discriminatory, and mean behavior.

In the workplace, it has to be no talk or behavior that is cheap, that is insulting, or that can lead to violence. The guideline at work: Keep your talk and your behavior focused on your job and on your success. Avoid the talk and the actions that could lead to a lawsuit.

NOODLES™

⌷$⌷ **Chapter 37** ⌷$⌷

No Overloading by Overanalysis

⌷$⌷ Computers make it easy to do a lot of things, but most of the things that make it easier to do don't need to be done.

—Andy Rooney

---

79. No tendency charts.
80. No computer analysis.
81. No coaches on phones in press box.

In Sports

Tendency is big with coaches. "They scout the other teams and they talk about what you might call the other teams' habits," John explains. "What's their tendency to do on the goal line, on third-'n'-five, all those kinds of things the team usually has done." Not John. "We don't have a chart. We don't really keep track of much of that." Why? He laughs, "We just are ready for everything."

"You know," he says, "there's a lot of buzzwords in everything. Education's big on it. In coaching it's really big. And *tendency*, that's one of the buzzwords."

John is just as dismissive of headphones in the press box and computer analysis.

About coaches on phones in the press box, he says, "We think we can do as much from the sidelines." He adds, "What's our record again? I think we've won 96 games in the last 10 years. We shouldn't have won any because we don't use anyone on headphones in the press box, and the other teams do. Obviously it doesn't matter."

As for computer analysis, he says, "Some teams are BIG on putting everything into a computer and then spitting out so damn much information that you can't begin to use it." John came close to doing the same. He likes to work with his computer, he does spreadsheets, he's intrigued by all the things computers can do. But, to use it for analysis, he draws the line. "Somebody's got to spend a lot of time putting in the information. That's going to be me, you know. I'm not looking for more work. I'm looking to lessen my load. And be more effective. Just creating more work for yourself doesn't make you more effective."

In the Workplace

It's NO to overpreparation and overanalysis. It's NO to wasting money on one too many employees counting paper clips when no paper clips really need counting. It's NO to adding more computers and computer power in your work area when what you already have serves you just fine. It's NO to new technology just because the new technology is available.

At Employers of America, we have no automatic telephone answering system during business hours and no voice mail. I put electronic phone-answering and voice mail right up where John puts tendency charts and coaches on headphones. Customers and clients want personal contact when they call. And if that's what customers and clients want, it's the most effective approach in your business or organization to give them the service they want.

In your workplace, what are the *tendency charts?* What is the wasteful *computer analysis?* Who are the drones on phones in their *press boxes?* Where is the wasted effort you and others could eliminate and then invest more effectively?

$ Chapter 38 $

No Fear of Taking a Risk

$ Never let the fear of striking out get in your way.

—Babe Ruth

---

85. No belief that aggressive teams get penalties.

In Sports

"*Physical.* That's a buzzword. You've got to be *physical.* I don't even know for sure what it means," John laughs. "I think it means damn mean." Then John talks about the dirtiest coach he's ever faced. He believes this guy actually coached his players on how to seriously hurt opposing players without the officials seeing it. Then he adds, "But some of the dirtiest teams usually are the lousiest."

He notes there is a difference between dirty teams, teams with players who intentionally do physical harm, and teams that are aggressive. "Some think that to be aggressive you have to break rules and have penalties. We don't believe that. If you get penalties you don't under-

> ⎿$⎤ I don't get angry. I get aggressive.
>
> —Joseph A. McDonnell, CEO, iShopSecure

stand the rules. We're trying to avoid penalties, but that doesn't mean you can't be aggressive."

In the Workplace

Like many coaches, for a few years John sold insurance part-time. Talking about being aggressive without penalties, he observes: "When I was an insurance salesman, you'd push but you wouldn't misrepresent. You'd give 'em every opportunity to say 'No,' and you'd push and do as much as you can, but you didn't lie. You're truthful."

A couple months ago, I did a guest teacher stint with a business ethics class at an area college. I acknowledged that most people believe *business ethics* is an oxymoron, and the 27 students agreed. In fact, initially in the discussion every student who spoke up cited bitter, cynical experiences with *business*. Blatantly untruthful, unethical, and aggressive marketing and selling tactics have conditioned buyers to distrust all commercial activity.

But we can't let our revulsion with unethical commercial behavior keep us from pursuing our own day-to-day victories in life and in work. My economics professor at Saint John's, when I was a student there, was John (Johnny Blood) McNally (star running back for the Green Bay Packers, player-coach for the Pittsburgh Steelers, and John Gagliardi's predecessor as coach at Saint John's). McNally started *every* class by walking in, stepping to the blackboard, picking up a piece of chalk, and drawing a baseball diamond. As each lecture proceeded, no matter what the

> |$| A "no" uttered from the deepest conviction is better
> |T| than a "yes" merely uttered to please, or what is worse,
> to avoid trouble.
>
> —Mahatma Gandhi

economics topic, McNally used baseball activity to explain the principles of economics. At the time, I thought it was pretty dumb to try to explain all economics as a baseball game. But through the years, McNally's lessons have made some sense to me.

And today McNally's metaphor, I believe, is a good one. For example, one of the excitements in baseball is anticipating a runner stealing bases—watching for and anticipating the contest, the game of wits, between the pitcher and the runner. In life and in work activities, we gain satisfaction, even pleasure, from being aggressive and winning. Few people win without taking risks.

What's important is knowing that we can be aggressive and take risks without crossing the illegal and unethical lines and getting penalized.

⌊$⌋ **Chapter 39** ⌊$⌋

No Giving Power to Setbacks

⌊$⌋ In organizations we often believe mistakes are a
problem. But mistakes are not the problem. They're just
natural. It is how we respond when they occur that can
be a "problem" because our response reveals our
character and the outer limits (at that moment) of how
much we can achieve.

—Carol S. Pearson, senior editor, *The Inner Edge*

---

91. *No dwelling on bad things.*

In Sports

"We take the game seriously, but we don't live and die over
it," John says. "I don't think it's life and death. We don't
like to lose any more than my mother doesn't like to have a
cake or spaghetti sauce turn out bad. Who likes anything
going wrong?"

But John doesn't dwell on the bad things. He does joke
about it. "They ask me if I think about retirement. I say, 'No,
I never think about retirement but I do think about suicide
every time we lose.' "

I protest, "No, you don't really do *that!*"

"Yah, I like to kid around with our players, and they're
always asking me about certain jokes, they want to hear
'em again."

$\boxed{\$}$ The Success Equation begins with employees, today more commonly called "associates." A restaurant manager we know put it this way, "It's funny, but true. The better I treat my associates the better they treat the guests—and the healthier the bottom line is. . . ." Both academic research and personal experience validate the conclusion that associate success drives individual and organizational success.

—James A. Belasco and Jerre Stead, *Soaring with the Phoenix*

John turns serious. "The only way I can continue coaching for this length of time is not to dwell on success and failure. The secret is somehow you have to put all that, success and failure, behind you. Either way, wins or losses, you've got to forget about it. And get on. You can't live in the past at all. Learn from the past, but get ready for tomorrow. Once that Saturday's [game] is over, well it's DONE. We can't change it one way or the other. So you've got to forget about it."

In the Workplace

When the bad happens, John says, "Learn the lesson from it, then forget it. We tell our guys, 'Think happy thoughts. Think pleasant thoughts.' Sounds kind of childish. But we tell 'em, 'Try to think of something good, accentuate the positive.' "

It *does* sound kind of childish. Think positive. Think happy. But coming from the most successful active coach in college football, with memories of more than 50 years of record-setting coaching to draw on, it is said with authority.

Not just *remembering*, but *recalling* and *rehashing* the bad things, is probably the worst drain on the energies of people in your workplace. Human brains evolved with built-in danger-avoidance programming. Thinking of our brains as mega-chip computers (an imperfect metaphor, to be sure), our brains have a built-in *anti-virus* program that is constantly scanning for danger. When we are infants and children, our parents, our siblings, our playmates, and countless others keep upgrading this anti-virus program in our brains, filling it with more and more dangers. So too many adults go to their workplaces with their brains hardwired to focus on the negatives.

Your jobs as workplace coach are to keep your own mental power focused on the opportunities, on the possibilities, and to do everything you possibly can to focus your associates' and employees' minds on opportunities and possibilities.

⌐$⌐ Chapter 40 ⌐$⌐

No Settling for Less Than the Best

⌐$⌐ Defense is not talent. It's attitude and pride.

> —June Olkowski, women's basketball coach,
> Northwestern University

---

95. *No study or tutoring necessary.*

In Sports

Many schools have a compulsory study session for their athletes. John has no quarrel with that. But it isn't needed at Saint John's. "We get smart kids," he says. "You should see their grade point averages. They're high. Our football players, they're very good students. They don't need compulsory study or tutoring. A kid can't get in here anymore unless he's a very good student."

In the Workplace

Now here's a challenge! In a tight labor market, many employers have to hire people who are unprepared, who need plenty of training and learning time. So what's the answer?

⌊$⌋ I played baseball, football, and basketball. Every time I
ㅜ walked onto a field or a court, I expected to be a
winner—not because of the final score of the game,
but because I had played my best.

—Gregory Guice: At age four, in an iron lung with polio,
today a Unity minister, named one of the top 10 teachers in
the nation by *Ebony* magazine in 1988

Hire people for their brains. Hire people for their willingness to apply themselves. In sports, it's called *heart*. Hire people who will be aggressive in using their minds and talents to win on the job.

A small-town newspaper publisher believed in me and gave me my start in writing for pay, even though I wasn't prepared. He needed a sports editor. I had no experience. He hired me just the same. He put me under the supervision of an editor who had recently graduated from journalism school. The editor allowed me all the time I needed to write and rewrite my stories. He critiqued them and gave me the time to rewrite them. It's a model of coaching employees I've used through all my years as a supervisor and an employer.

Hire good people, smart people. Then give them the time, tools, and coaching they need to succeed. Call it on-the-job tutoring. John won't quarrel with that. (Just don't use the buzzword *mentoring*.)

⌊$⌋ Chapter 41 ⌊$⌋

No Promises. Just Results.

⌊$⌋ At the College of Saint Benedict, our student-athletes learn lessons on the court and playing field that they will take with them for life. From being a team player to knowing how to think quickly under pressure, women student-athletes are prepared for the challenges that business provides because they've experienced them before.

—Carol Howe-Veenstra, head volleyball coach and athletic director, College of Saint Benedict, St. Joseph, Minnesota

97. *No player has NOT graduated. (Almost all in four years.)*
98. *No player lost through ineligibility.*
99. *No discipline problems.*
100. *No senior class has NOT had a prospective pro football player.*
101. *No senior class has NOT had players accepted to medical, law, or other graduate schools.*
102. *No other college team in history averaged 61.5 points a game—the NCAA record.*
103. *No wider point margin in national playoff history.*
104. *No team has fewer injuries.*

> [$] The man who gives up accomplishes nothing and is only a hindrance. The man who does *not* give up can move mountains.
>
> —Ernest Hello, 19th-century French philosopher and essayist

105. No small college coach has won more games (second most in history).
106. No small college team has had more national media coverage.
107. No promises. Just results.

In Sports

John never asks if a young man is big enough to play a position. He asks only if the man is good enough. The results show he's right. Because of his high standards and his smart coaching, he attracts good men. These good young men produce the results.

Some coaches will take issue with at least a few of John's NOs. He recalls speaking to coaches just after winning a national championship. "One of the coaches speaks up and says it's hard for them to accept certain things. Like not tackling in practice and like not having a coach in the press box. He says, 'Don't you think you'd of done better?' I say, 'Let me think about that. Okay, we just won a national championship. We played 12 games and we won 'em all. I don't know how the hell we could win 13. We only played 12. We scored like 62 points a game. We led the nation in scoring. One team, Duluth, they were the second-place team in the league. We beat 'em 63 to 7. I guess we could have beaten them 85 to nothing, but 63 to 7 was pretty good.' "

Amazing results, by what one sports writer calls "the finest and most innovative mind in all of collegiate football."

In the Workplace

The secret to Saint John's football success is simple: good players, with innovative coaching, who work smart, not mean. Apply this formula in the workplace: Hire good people, people with brainpower and a strong work ethic, a willingness to apply themselves. Create an innovative culture and environment. Be willing to do things differently. Lead smart, coach smart, and work smart.

And, then, get out of the way. Unlike most football coaches, John doesn't call many of the plays. The Saint John's quarterback calls the plays 90% or more of the time. And, when John sends in a play, it's more of a suggestion. His quarterbacks are matching wits with the opposing coaches—and winning 75% of the time.

The smart workplace coach leads by hiring the best and then gets out of the way.

[$] Chapter 42 [$]

No End to the Possibilities

[$] The best leaders rejuvenate the system instead of preserve the status quo.

—Ann Richards, former Texas governor

---

108. No end to the possibilities of more NOs.

In Sports

John's better approach to coaching started with his experiencing some really bad coaching.

It started with his high school coach. This man was just the opposite of the coach John became. His high school coach was a great punter. He hogged the ball, loved to punt, punted the ball all over the stadium. "Well, I was the punter and he wasn't showing me," John begins the story. "I couldn't punt half as well as he could. But he wouldn't show me. But he didn't punt in the game, I had to punt the ball in the game. I couldn't call the coach in to punt."

John was a junior in high school. "We had a lousy team. We'd call a play, I'd hear the lineman say, 'Who do I block?' " John laughs telling it. "I'm going to get killed out there. . . . But, boy, we were working hard in practice, chasing the coach's punts, hard, stupid things, no correlation to the game. The game starts, the lineman says, 'Who do I block?' The ball's coming to me." Again John laughs. "No wonder I was getting killed."

Then the coach is drafted into World War II and John (he's only 16) takes over the coaching. "Well, I want to make sure these guys know who to block."

From that day on, for John there's been no end to his NOs. There's been no end to his growth. No end to the possibilities.

In the Workplace

These NOs are great. But there is no end to more YESs, also. John isn't saying no end to more negatives; he's saying no end to more innovations.

This morning I sat in with a hiring committee for a non-profit agency, interviewing an applicant for the executive position. We asked him for his ideas on innovations for the agency. He offered some ideas and then said, "I always think there is a better way." In the workplace, that's called continuous improvement.

And don't forget having fun. No end to the possibilities of having more fun while the work gets done.

$ Part III $

NO-How Coaching and You

⌊$⌋ Chapter 43 ⌊$⌋

YESs and NOs at Work

The Profitmaker's Job Description

⌊$⌋ Once you get your life focused in a way that works for you, you need to apply a very important skill: saying no to something before you say yes to something else. Whenever you say yes, you must say no to something else.

—Jennifer White, author of *Work Less, Make More*, founder of the JWC Group

---

Notice how many people in the work world start each day with a Bad Day drill. Imagine the impact on your lives if you and your associates and employees had a Beautiful Day "calisthenic" break periodically. Instead of dredging up what's wrong, share what's right, what's nice, about the day.

In fact, take a little time with your associates and employees and identify a few of the YESs and NOs in your business or organization that help you win.

At Employers of America, we actually sign a commitment, a pledge to do all we can to perform 10 YESs and to avoid 10 NOs. We call them The Profitmaker's Job Description. John Gagliardi doesn't believe in job descriptions, but we believe our Profitmaker's Job Description is an exception. Here is our list:

The 10 YESs

YES to Excellence. My job—in all that I do and in every detail—is to deliver excellence . . . in ways that contribute to profits!

YES to Opportunity. I'll look at every problem as an opportunity. By looking for opportunities I'll discover solutions.

YES to Brainpower. I'll use my brain's power to improve the quality of what I do, to improve the quality of what everyone does here, and to improve our profits . . . by looking for solutions and by coming up with new ideas.

YES to Honesty. I'll be so honest with myself and with others that everyone can totally count on my word and I can count on the word of others.

YES to Accountability. If I screw up I'll acknowledge it, at least to myself, and go back and do it right.

YES to Focusing. I'll be 100% mentally and emotionally present when I am at work. I'll be at work with a full cup of energy, interest, enthusiasm and commitment to focus on doing my job well.

YES to Communicating. When there is something in my job or in the workplace that is bothering me . . . or something I see that is interfering with my doing my work well . . . I'll talk about this in a positive, constructive way with the people involved. When I see an opportunity to improve profits by improving what I or anyone else does here, I'll speak up. I'll willingly share what I think.

YES to Learning More. I'll gain more knowledge and skill. I'll make myself more valuable. More valuable to my employer. More valuable to myself. I can never know enough.

YES to Improving. I'll be open to constructive guidance. I'll hear feedback willingly and act positively on what I hear.

YES to Fun. If I'm not having some fun doing what I do, it isn't worth striving to make more profits. So I'll make some fun happen, too.

The 10 NOs

NO to Negative Talk about myself (saying things like "I can't do that. I was always dumb at . . .").

NO to Negative Talk about my co-workers and others.

NO to Gossiping about my co-workers and about others. If I can't say something good or constructive about someone I won't say anything at all.

NO to Negative Talk about present and prospective members. After all, all my income and benefits come from them.

NO to Being Satisfied with doing a task less than well done.

NO to Freezing at the Roadblocks in my job. When I'm up against what looks like a roadblock, I'll look for the possibilities . . . to break through, tunnel under, go around, or fly over!

NO to Talking About a problem. I'll see it as a challenge and focus, instead, on overcoming the challenge.

NO to Blaming Others. I'll let go of judging others. I'll lift up others instead.

NO to "Stirring the Pot." I'm here together with others each day to have some fun and to make and improve our profits and opportunities . . . by doing everything I can to make our members' and prospective members' jobs as employers, managers and supervisors easier, less stressful and more enjoyable! I'm not here to create stress for myself or for others.

NO to Being a Grouch. I'll put on cheerfulness instead.

⎣$⎦ **Chapter 44** ⎣$⎦

Your Winning NOs and YESs

The genius of John Gagliardi's NOs list is that it runs counter to our culture's self-centered permissiveness. Our media and our culture condition people to believe that each of us is entitled to get 15 minutes of fame *every day!* Without effort, without discipline, without commitment.

I don't believe that slapping up The 10 Commandments on the wall will change anyone's behavior. I don't believe that posting The Profitmaker's Job Description will automatically turn a workplace into a great place to work. And I don't believe you can simply choose five or 10 of John's NOs, hand them out to your team or to your associates and employees, and expect a transformation.

In the workplace, for instance, leaders and their employees don't always see eye-to-eye on everything. According to International Survey Research, a Chicago polling firm, a 1998 survey of about 460,000 employees and managers showed that 73% of the senior managers said their firm encouraged employees to give their best, but only 51% of the employees agreed. The survey also showed that 66% of the senior managers said their firm established a climate where people can challenge the traditional way of doing things, but only 49% of their employees agreed.

But think of the value in identifying and publicizing the core YESs and NOs that reflect your team's or your workforce's environment and culture and that are keys to your and their success.

Here's a suggestion: Share John's Winning NOs with your team members or your workforce. Share the Profitmaker's Job Description. (You might give each person a copy of this book.) Then ask them for their suggestions for the YESs and NOs that they believe are the keys to their winning.

With their input, put together your own list of five, 10, or 20 YESs and NOs. And don't just post your list somewhere, where it's ignored. Live it.

⊢$⊣ Chapter 45 ⊢$⊣

Coaching

It's Tougher Than Always Winning

⊢$⊣ I see challenges as opportunities to learn and stretch
beyond limitations I have placed on myself or others
have placed on me.

—Adapted from *Daily Word,* January 16, 1999

If you read the sports pages to get your guidance on winning, *look out!*

Why? Because, contrary to what so many sports
coaches keep pounding home, winning isn't everything. In
no sports can you win every game or contest. In business,
you can't win every sale. In fact, in business you usually
lose more sales than you win.

So there has to be something fundamentally wrong
with today's *winning is everything* creed.

Several years ago, Jimmy Johnson, then Dallas Cowboys coach, called a Fort Worth radio program—just before
the NFC title game against the 49ers—and boasted: "We
will win the ballgame. And you can put it in three-inch
headlines. We will win the ballgame."

$ We all play golf, we all have a bug. We're all trying to get better somehow. I'm going to continue to work on my whole game.

—Tiger Woods, after winning the 100th U.S. Open

If you set the same impossible day-in, day-out standard for yourself, and for your team members, you are doomed to fail.

James Miller (honored as executive of the year by the office products industry) and Paul B. Brown (assistant managing editor of *Financial World*) included good pointers on this topic in their book *The Corporate Coach*. When I read Coach Johnson's brag, I thought of the following advice from Miller and Brown's book: "Under-promise, over-deliver. There is a natural tendency to brag about your people and your company. After all, you're proud that you routinely do the impossible. But be careful—customers take you at your word. . . . Always build in a bit of a cushion, so you can do what you say you will."

There is coaching that turns players and employees into life-long winners. And there is coaching that turns out arrogant loud-mouths.

Bernie Lincicome, writing in the *Chicago Tribune*, had this comment on Coach Johnson's insufferable braggadocio: "The Cowboys are full of the same stuff that so endeared the University of Miami to the nation when Johnson coached there—insolence, arrogance, ego and immense ability."

At about the same time that Coach Johnson was mouthing off in Texas, Buffalo Bills coach Marv Levy offered a better model of coaching for all of us who coach, in sports and in the workplace. With the Bills making a habit of getting trashed in the Super Bowl, Coach Levy said, "You have to get ready and continue the quest for what we've just fallen short of."

In sports and in your workplace, winning means *you have to continue the quest.*

INDEX

$

ABOUT THE AUTHOR

|$|

Jim Collison is president of Employers of America, the national association for employers, managers, and supervisors.

Jim's workworld experience began with selling the *Minneapolis Star* on the streets in Blue Earth, Minnesota, when he was eight years old. By the time he was 14, he had his own newspaper route and his own office (two orange crates in the basement) and was managing other carriers for the *St. Paul Pioneer-Press*. At 19, he was assistant foreman on a crew of field workers in southern Minnesota. A few years later, after a stint as sports editor of two southern Minnesota weeklies (in Blue Earth), and after graduating from Saint John's University (in Collegeville, Minnesota), he started a newspaper and job printing business.

For the past 23 years, Jim has headed Employers of America. He is author of *The Complete Suggestion Program Made Easy, The Complete Employee Handbook Made Easy,*

Skill-Building in Advanced Reading, and *Mental Power in Reading.* He is senior editor of *Smart Workplace Practices* newsletter.

You can reach the author by calling 800-728-3187 or at his e-mail address: employer@employerhelp.org.

ABOUT
EMPLOYERS OF AMERICA

Employers of America, the national association founded by employers in 1976, helps employers, managers, and supervisors make their HR work a lot easier.

You can get all kinds of employer-friendly information, HR help, and profit-boosting tools at the association's web site: www.employerhelp.org.

Jim Collison, president of Employers of America, is available to speak and to provide training on these and similar topics:

- NO-How Coaching for Leaders: Strategies for Winning in Your Workplace
- NO-How Coaching for the Soul: Step-by-Step to Personal Happiness . . . Starting Right Now
- NO End to the Possibilities: Unleashing Your Genius to Invent Your Success

- Profit Power at Work: Unleashing Your Employees' Brain Power with a Suggestion Program Made Easy
- Profit-Is-Job-1: How to Unleash Your Employee's Profitmaking Power

If you're interested in arranging for a speaker, a workshop, or on-site training on NO-How Coaching in the workplace, or similar success-in-the-workplace topics, please call Employers of America at 800-728-3187. Or e-mail employer@employerhelp.org.